Lynette,

I pry for a Bless[...]
By Every week with [...]
He makes it Plan from [...]
heart to [...].

Blessings

# Some Things Made Plain

## Theresa Kirk

For information regarding permission or additional copies, contact the publisher:

**KNOWLEDGE POWER BOOKS**

A Division of Knowledge Power Communications, Inc.
25379 Wayne Mills Place, Suite 131
Valencia, CA 91355
www.knowledgepowerbooks.com


Edited by:
Gena Clayton


Jacket Design and Photography:
Juan Roberts of Creative Lunacy
CreativeLunacy1.blogspot.com


Library of Congress Control Number: 2010938173

ISBN 978-0-9818790-2-4

Printed in China

*A Gift To*

_____

*From*

_____

# Some Things Made Plain

# THE ART OF
# CHELSEA LAURICE KIRK

*Psalm 127:3 (K J V)*
*Lo, children are an heritage of the LORD: and the fruit of the womb is his reward.*

*Psalm 127:3 (Amplified Bible)*
*Behold, children are a heritage from the Lord, the fruit of the womb a reward.*

I want the World to see what my heritage looks like. Father I thank You for the Art of Chelsea. Phum, thank you for staying up all night, when we were no longer able to find the original, but then like me you started from scratch, now look at your masterpiece. Well I kept my promise, that you would be a part of my 1st book. Now the world will see part of the legacy that was fashioned in my womb, with an amazing gift/talent.

*Proverbs 22:6 (Amplified Bible)*
*Train up a child in the way he should go [and in keeping with his individual gift or bent], and when he is old he will not depart from it.*

I love you, and bless God He trust your Pappy & I to lead you
      *….. Mommy*

# CONTENTS

# DEDICATION

## In the Spirit:

I dedicate my knowledge to the only wise God, because I know that if He decided not to let me in on His hidden mysteries this would not have been possible.

## In the Natural:

This volume of *Some Things Made Plain,* dedicated to my sister, Pastor Angela Nichols, for our lunch date that chilly day in November, when I was certain you were off just a tad. Sissy, thank you, for your sensitivity in the spirit which has proved to be accurate. I have told you for years if I could just have a taste of the anointing on your life. Today I get it. If I had tried to be you I would have forfeited the knowledge of this project.

I love you *forever* & ever ~ TeeCee

To reader that desires to go from daunting to plain....I *dedicat*e this one to you as well.

Blessings Today & Forever,

Theresa Kirk
Author

# ACKNOWLEDGEMENTS

### 1 Corinthians 2:9-12 (KJV)

*But as it is written, Eye hath not seen, nor ear heard, neither have entered into the heart of man, the things which God hath prepared for them that love him.*

*But God hath revealed them unto us by his Spirit: for the Spirit searcheth all things, yea, the deep things of God.*

*For what man knoweth the things of a man, save the spirit of man which is in him? Even so the things of God knoweth no man, but the Spirit of God.*

*Now we have received, not the spirit of the world, but the spirit which is of God; that we might know the things that are freely given to us of God.*

Giving all Glory to my Lord and Savior Jesus Christ, for it is only through His willingness to impart wisdom that this book has been made possible. To my amazing husband-prayer partner-and my absolute best friend Mr. Ron Kirk, thank you baby for letting me stay up late to achieve my dream. To my beautiful children, Chelsea and Jaylon for letting me, even when I knew you did not want to read my material but just did it because it was Mommy asking, thank you. My mother Ellinor Nelson, your shoulder was not in vain. My Moto in the person of Mrs. LaDonna Hughley, there are no words for what God has given us as friends, I thank Him daily. Cherie Sellers thanks for tag teaming with me. Divine Divas Inc., you cheerleaders/prayer warriors, I am blessed you all are wonderful to me. Ms. Regina Clayton, reading my stuff with exceeding joy even in the snow (Naomi & Ruth), and in the end of this project became my ultimate editor. To my awesome Pastors Dr. Fred Hodge & Pastor Linda Hodge at Living Praise Christian center for all your prayers and the LPCC family. For all those whose name I did not mention, please do not count it against my heart but my lack of sleep while preparing this book. A special "thank you" to Evangelist Byrd for pointing me in the right direction that lead me to Mrs. Willa Robinson and for taking my book to the river every time you went there to pray.

I love you all and pray that your lives are blessed as mine was every time HE made SOME THINGS PLAIN for me to share with you....

Theresa Kirk
Author

# ENTHUSIAM AND PRAISE

First impressions are everything to me. I will never forget when I met Theresa Kirk, over 20 years ago. We met at church just praising the Lord in a mighty way, and the Word that Sunday was even better. We have been praising the Lord from that day until now, and have no plans on stopping anytime soon. We have been sista-friends every since our 1st encounter and we have been inseparable. Both of us raising babies at that time, family are what we shared. We went on walks, had many talks about husbands, children, cooking, and some kind of way we always ended up with the Word as our favorite topic. It was evident early on to me, that Theresa was a woman after Gods heart; she is wise beyond her years. She is a woman of her word; her relationship with God is of the utmost importance to her. She is a lady in every since of the word, and an asset to all who know her. Her family, Ron, Chelsea and Jaylon are an encouragement to all who witness their family dynamics. All of the Kirks support the ministry in some fashion. There is a great truth in the statement "A Family that pray's together stays together." This is a daily practice in the Kirk home. I honor my "Sista-Friend" Theresa Kirk, and I celebrate her for accomplishing the task that God set before her. "Some Things Made Plain" is a wonderful book.

**I am very proud of you, Congratulations ~ LaDonna Y. Hughley**

Reading this marvelous work by Minister Theresa Kirk has been an amazingly heartwarming experience. Her creative insight engages you and provides the much-needed encouragement for today's life as a believer. Theresa uses seemingly insignificant everyday occurrences to connect with the reader and she assists us in making sense of the simplistic ways in which Christ conveys His love and everlasting care. Each entry is truly inspirational and stirs the heart to apply godly wisdom to the days' challenges. As a people, we desire to be affirmed in our homes, in our work and in our calling. This devotional provokes feelings of empowerment while humbly reminding us that God is intimately concern with every facet of our lives. It provides a deeply meaningful understanding of God's love combined with a healthy love for one self and others. Timely and purposeful, Theresa has listened to the guidance of the Holy Spirit in writing a devotional for 21st century women and the generation to come.

Blessings to you as you indulge yourself into this decidedly stimulating reading. **Mrs. Donna M. Hunter, MA**

I am very proud of the author of this book Theresa Kirk. She is my friend, sister and a true example of a mature Godly woman whom I love dearly. God has given her the gift of knowledge, to dissect His word and encourage others with the awesome revelation she receives. . As she meditates through prayer, fasting and sitting at His feet, He gives her some powerful insights on how it applies to the realities of life. Some Things Made Plain will cause you to grasp hold to a deeper sense of perspective for your life. God's word is a "lamp unto my feet, and a light unto my path" (Psalm 119:105). When we allow God's word to rule every area of our lives, it shines bright on every situation, conflict, and trial, and it gives us the insights we need to make the right decisions and choices through life. I am a witness that Theresa has put God first in her life as He instructed her to write this book. I pray that as you read each page along with your Bible, it will encourage your heart and you will trust God even more.

**Cherie Sellers**

I have been a student of Theresa Kirk's amazing teachings for more years than I care to count. She has guided me, enlightened me, and prayed for me and I am a better Christian, mother and friend because of her. This book is just the beginning of an amazing journey for all who read it and will continue to read her works. She has an amazing gift of simplicity and clarity when delivering God's word. Your understanding of him and his plan for your life will forever be cemented in your spirit as you journey through the wonderful writings my friend.

**Be Blessed ~ Edie D. Morris**

Woman of virtue, excellence, and character is the description of Minister Theresa Kirk. She is a woman of God who loves the people of God and cares about them. I have seen her overcome many obstacles in life, but she kept her eyes on the Lord and his promises. In addition, the Lord delivered her out of them all. As you read this devotional, allow the Holy Spirit to minister to you where you are right now, for I believe you will be truly blessed.

**Minister L'Tanya James ~ L.J.Ministries**

## CHAPTER ONE

# OUR LORD

## 2 Corinthians 3:17 (KJV)

*Now the Lord is that Spirit: and where the Spirit of the Lord is, there is liberty.*

KNOWING MY NAME MAKES US FAMILY

SAY THE NAME

THROTTLE

THE MINUTE TAKER

HE ANSWERS NOT IN A WHISPER

THIS IS CHRIST

RANSOM

PASSION OVER PRIDE

AMBER ALERT

CANNOT RENEGE

# KNOWING MY NAME MAKES US FAMILY

## Psalm 91:14 (NIV)

*"Because he loves me," says the LORD, "I will rescue him; I will protect him, for he acknowledges my name. He will call upon, Me and I will answer;"*

There is a lot to be said about family. A family has many dynamics. There is love, laughter, fights, madness, gladness, dinners, holidays, vacations, and then there are the nicknames. The interesting thing about nicknames is that generally you are only allowed to use them if you are in the family. To paint a picture of what I am saying, bring a friend to a holiday dinner and watch their facial expression, when a member of the family uses a term of endearment, often times they laugh, and for the analytical mind they inquire where, when, who, and does it mean something significant. Usually, if Grandma or Grandpa is present, they begin to shed some light on the history of your nickname.

The description can be cute, funny, or even tough if it describes what you use to be or use to do. For me, mine is TC, why? Because my mother called me as an infant Tucca, and Great-Grandma shortened it by just saying TC. My mother use to say Tucca described to her just how cute I was. Well I am 42, and while I still explain the 3 w's to those who are not in the family, once they are privileged to know that part of my history, I consider them apart of my family. The best part for me really, is how I love to hear the way my mother explains the name. The awesome thing about the names of Jesus/ God is they can't be changed, or shortened but in everyway you say one of HIS names, they validate who HE is, and in all cases what we need. And like my mother, to her at that time in my life, it validated to her who I was.

**Definition of nickname: A descriptive, formal, or affectionate name used in place of the name most often called or used.**

**Are you in the family?**

# SAY THE NAME

## Proverbs 3:13 (NKJV)

*Happy is the man, who finds wisdom,*
*and the man who gains understanding.*

## *Jesus:*

The Alpha & Omega
Lord God
The Almighty
Son of Man
The First and the Last
The Living One
Son of God
Witness
Creator
Lion of the tribe of Judah
Root of David
Lamb
Shepherd
Christ
Faithful and True
Word of God
King of Kings
Lord of Lords
The morning Star
Emmanuel
The last Adam
His Anointed
Messiah
Rose of Sharon
Balm of Gilead

Ransom
Advocate
Wonderful
Redeemer
Shiloh
Jehovah
Strong Tower
Excellent
Judge
Our Potter
Master
Holy One
Carpenter
Son of MAN
The WORD
The Highest
Mediator
Intercessor
I AM
Kinsman
Hiding place
Faithful & True
Bread
King
Nazarene
Rod
Rabbi
Jesus Christ

*"When we know HIM by name, we should come to understand who HE is"*

**Do you know HIM by all names?**

# THROTTLE
### Ephesians 3:20 (NKJV)

*Now to Him who is able to do exceedingly abundantly above all that we ask or think, according to the power that works in us,*

**Throttle:**
Is the valve that monitors the internal combustion to regulate the amount of fuel or steam entering into the cylinders (mind).

**Throttle:**
To regulate speed by strangling or choking it to prevent disaster.

**Definition:** Choke. **Antonyms:** Free, release **Synonyms:** silence; smother; strangle; stifle

1. Alpha & Omega ~ **the First and the Last ~ the Beginning & the End**
2. Jehovah- Jireh ~ **Provider**
3. Elohim ~ **Strong**
4. El-Shaddai ~ **God all Sufficient**
5. Adonai ~ **Master**
6. Jehovah-Rophe ~ **Healing**
7. Jehovah-M'Kaddesh~ **Lord who sanctifies**
8. Jehovah-Nissi ~ **Our Banner**
9. Jehovah-Shalom ~ **Our Peace**
10. Jehovah-Rohi ~ **Our Shepherd**
11. Jehovah-Shammah ~ **The Lord always there**
12. Jehovah-Tsidkenu ~ **Our Righteousness**
13. El-Elyon ~ **Most High**

**"It is comforting knowing that for every trial that we may encounter, there is a Name that suits our very need, in times of trouble the key is to use them."**

## ~ I AM that I AM ~

# THE MINUTE TAKER

## Malachi 3:16 (MSG)

*Then those whose lives honored God got together and talked it over. God saw what they were doing and listened in. A book was opened in God's presence and minutes were taken of the meeting, with the names of the God-fearers written down, all the names of those who honored God's name.*

Can you imagine that all the times we sat around talking about our awesome Lord; He sat in and took minutes? That's right; He recorded our very words in His book of remembrance. So let me ask you what other topics could you sit around and get credit for? Our God is so full of mercy and grace we actually get credit for chatting about Him. **Selah**

Serving God means putting Him first and when we do, it honors Him, promotes who He is and proves we are grateful for what He has done for us, speaks volumes to those who listen, but ultimately proves we Believe. Get chatting credit.

### What is your credit like with the Master?

# HE ANSWERS NOT IN A WHISPER

## Psalm 3:3 (MSG)

*But you, GOD, shield me on all sides;*
*You ground my feet, you lift my head high;*
*With all my might I shout up to God,*
*His answers thunder from the holy mountain.*

Take a moment and really get this revelation in your spirit. The Creator of both heaven and earth is your shield.

A shield is defined as a safeguard, protector, buckler, buffer, cover, absorber, security. This is David's cry for help while on the run from his son, Absalom. Imagine if you will for just a moment that these are all the attributes of GOD in your time of trouble. There are times when we just want to throw in the towel. Instead, just shout to the One who will send your answer to your plea for help in a thunderous voice. Thunder--crashing; booming; loud; very loud; at full volume; rowdy; vociferous; penetrating. The powerful act in all this is when the help arrives, there is no doubt WHO rescued you, because your feet were grounded at the place where you cried out, and your head was lifted up. You not only heard, but you were able to see because of your stance.

> **"Stay grounded, and listen intently so when your protector sends the rowdy answer from the Holy mountain you are in the right place to be set free."**

# RANSOM

## Mark 10: 45 (NIV)

*"For even the Son of Man did not come to be served, but to serve,*
*and to give His life a ransom for many."*

### Ransom:
### A fee paid to free a slave or hostages
### The release of a person in return for payment

Jesus paid a ransom for us because we could not pay it ourselves. In His death, He released us from our slavery to sin. The disciples thought that Jesus' power would save them from Rome, but Jesus said His ***death*** would save them from sin and even greater, slavery.

We have all at some point seen movies where someone is taken hostage. In a particular scene, the S.W.A.T (Spiritual Weapons Against Terror) team is summoned to the location where the enemy is set up. Depending on how much danger the hostage may be in, a negotiator is called, in hopes of convincing the captor to free his hostage (prisoner/captive/slave) in exchange for some agreed upon security, usually money, property or in rare occasions, another person. Once ***RANSOM*** is paid, freedom is granted.

In these melodramas, the heroes receive applause and much appreciation from the hostage's family, and maybe even a few thanks from friends for the heroic stance they took.

The exciting reality, is that Jesus' reward for giving his life on the CROSS, was far greater than any applause or heartfelt gratitude that anyone could give. He now takes His seat at the right hand of the Father, whose expectations He granted, when He took our place, so he could deliver us from sin and death.

"The negotiation took place in Gethsemane and the ***Ransom*** was the ***CROSS.***"

# PASSION OVER PRIDE

### Matthew 27:11-14 (NKJV)

*Now Jesus stood before the governor. And the governor asked Him saying, "Are you the King of the Jews?" Jesus said to him "It is as you say." And while He was being accused by the chief priest and elders, He answered nothing. Then Pilate said to Him, "Do you not hear how many things they testify against You?" But He answered him not one word and the governor marveled greatly.*

Take a moment to really stop and think about what Jesus did that day on Cavalry, besides take your place for the sin that we so willfully did on our own accord; He laid down His pride regardless of what He looked like when He stood there, against the name calling the spitting, the throwing of all the rocks, and being accused of what? Blasphemy? Simply saying that He was in fact the Christ? The religious leaders needed to make this false accusation against our Lord, for the ultimate fulfillment of the prophecy mentioned in the Old Testament book of **Isaiah 53:7(Amplified)** He was oppressed, [yet when] He was afflicted, He was submissive and opened not His mouth; like a lamb that is led to the slaughter, and as a sheep before her shearers is dumb, so He opened not His mouth.

  He knew who He was but most importantly, His design for you and I, His principle reason to walk among us in the flesh, die a humiliating death, all because of the expectation of His Father. So what would be the significance of debate? Sometimes, the most **profound (deep; heartfelt)** things are never spoken, but proven in our response. For when you know who you are, whose you are and truly know your destination, what words could be spoken? There went ***pride*** and in walked the ***passion***.

**"His passion for us allowed Him to forget His pride, and remember the expectation of the Father whom was waiting for Him in Glory."**

# AMBER ALERT

### Isaiah 62:12 (NIV)

*They shall call them the Holy People, the Redeemed of the Lord; and you shall be called Sought After, the City No Longer Deserted.*

Have you ever wondered how you were actually found?  Did it ever occur to you that maybe the Father in heaven sent ~ an amber alert ~ with your **name** posted in lights on every highway?

**The amber alert read:**  Person abducted into a life of sin, on her way to hell, quick, fast and in a hurry.  She is currently wearing addictive behavior and overwhelmed by rejection, which has increased her level of insecurity.  She was last seen in a vehicle moving on Hwy 2 nowhere fast.  Witnesses described the driver as being very **DARK.**  Another witness said there were others in the car that resembled **LIGHT.**  When seen, you are asked to immediately call the **WE-TIP** Hotline at (555) JC-Throne.  Angels standing by Heaven 24 hours a day.

**WE-TIP - War Engaged- To Initiate *Power***

**WE-TIP - Worship imposed to tear down iniquity for heavens purpose, promise and PRIZE.**

**Because we were sought after by the Most High, we shall be apprehended and brought into safety.  So not one angel shall rest until we obtain our purpose, and then, we shall receive our Prize.**

Ponder for a moment that HE took time out to decree an Amber Alert with your name on it, to bring you home…

# CANNOT RENEGE

## 2 Corinthians 1:20 (NKJV)

*For all the promises of God in Him are Yes, and in Him Amen,*
*to the glory of God through us.*

There are several wonderful things that we can all say about our Father, which is in heaven. The one thing I personally love the absolute most, is that He will never change His mind on what He promised. He promised from the start of creation, that we would daily see the sun, and at night we would see the moon and its companions, the stars. He also said "that weeping may endure for but a night, but joy comes in the morning." Think about it, when you have cried yourself into a bitter sleep, because of whatever has caused you grief, the One who is watching over you, never sleeps, nor slumbers, do you not find that what you left in your rest, was not as heavy when you lifted your head from your resting place? I count Him worthy for so much more. Nevertheless, I am optimistic at the end of any given day, and believe that all that He said He will do concerning me and those that diligently seek Him shall come to pass. The Word is so powerful, it shows us the many promises that He kept. Just look at Sarah, and Abraham, David, Naomi, and Ruth, Zachariah and Elizabeth, the children of Israel. My goodness, what promises have you witnessed or even experienced? How about these, mercies that are new everyday, peace that surpasses all your understanding, the blood that covers you and keeps you from really falling, or this one, the weapon can form, but it shall not in anyways prosper.

The God we serve is a Promise Keeper....so hold tight and wait to see your promises...I bet if you look up right now, there was one waiting for you ...GO get what's been promised, it is yours no one else can have it.

**He is faithful not to *RENEGE.***

# CHAPTER TWO

# COURAGE

## Deuteronomy 31:6 (NKJV)

*Be strong and of good courage, do not fear nor be afraid of them; for the LORD your God, He is the One who goes with you. He will not leave you nor forsake you."*

BEGGING IS NOT ALLOWED
MAKE A STRONG APPROACH
THE ROAD YOU ARE ON
SCARED TO LET IT GO
NO PHONE RECEPTION
ON TIME
VICTORY IS
MUST STAY FOCUSED

# BEGGING IS NOT ALLOWED

## Psalms 37:25(NKJV)

*I have been young, and now am old; Yet I have not seen the righteous forsaken, nor His descendants begging bread.*

Ok, time for honesty. Is it me or do you agree that, that dog gone beggin gets on your last nerve? Think about it, Mommmmmmy can I have one more? Your reply is what did I already say? Then comes your significant other, reminding you of the premises made to shuttle children from here to there, not to mention the raging hormones that lead to the batting of eyes that sometimes get stuck looking up at the ceiling! You're exasperated beyond mentioning, so you surrender and give in.

Something suddenly clicks in your brain and you remember the reason for your sound decision! My daughter Chelsea is 16 and my son Jaylon is 14. There is a good reason that God called me to be their parent. For all of their begging and pleading....I am the bottom dollar and the ultimate decision is mine, especially regarding balance for all parties involved.

I am confident that God's word is true. For He speaks to me daily...all day! When He tells me no, I must trust that He knows best. His promises are yes and Amen and he never changes His mind. God gives us that same ability regarding promises that we have made to Him regarding ourselves, our children and loved ones. In certain circumstances, we know best and that is that! So word to the wise my friends, when your heart and mind is in sync about a thing, don't change your mind, no matter the begging, so encourage loved ones....No Begging !

# MAKE A STRONG APPROACH

### Ephesians 3:12 (KJV)

*In whom we have boldness and access with confidence through faith in HIM.*

### (MSG)

*When we trust in Him, we are free to say whatever needs to be said,*
*Bold to go wherever we need to go.*

If the instructions are clear, why then do we tip-toe when we have been told what to do by the ONE who did it before us? HE said go with boldness and with confidence. Confidence will ensure that once we have what we desire, we will know how to make good use of what we have obtained. Think of it this way, you have put on your Sunday's best, you know you look fabulous, so when you hit the door there is an air about you, not arrogance, but because you took the necessary steps to look as fabulous as you feel, you are confident. So my brothers and my sisters go!

The Father wants us to know that He has equipped us with all that we need to be bold and confident. He proved this very thing when He took the keys from the enemy that could have kept us locked in the gates of hell forever. He showed us how to defeat the enemy--with confidence and with great boldness!

**"We have a manual, and the instructions are clear."**
**So make a strong approach~**

# THE ROAD YOU ARE ON

## Isaiah 51:10 (NKJV)

*Are You not the One who dried up the sea, The waters of the great deep; That made the depths of the sea a road, For the redeemed to cross over?*

If the road you are on does not lead you to GOD, then you are on the wrong road. If HE would divide the sea to get the ones HE called redeemed, then my friend know that there has been a road paved just for you to get to HIM. Find the road you need to be on to get to HIM. The authority we have been given by way of the Holy Ghost gives us an internal NAVIGATION system. Ask the maker how to activate it. In fact, check the owner's manual. Sometimes we are headed in the wrong direction, and may need to make a U-turn *(you turn)* in order for you get on the right path to your destination. Don't break any laws trying to get there; the penalty could be costly. So, read the signs, carefully—*yield* means slow down; *railroad crossing* means to watch out for the trains that may cross your path; *stop* just means *stop*.

**John 14:6 (KJV) Jesus said, I am the way, the truth, and the life: no man cometh to the Father, but by me.**

Here are some other signs to look for on your journey—dead end (this way leads to nowhere); slippery when wet (be careful, or you may fall); winding road/sharp curves (slow down and proceed with caution), wrong way (turn around, go in the other direction). Then there are regulatory and guide signs: Construction/ maintenance ahead (slow down, read the Word, fast and pray); REST AREA (Rest on God's Promises). Your safety and the safety of others depends on you taking heed to all road signs.

**"If you're a new driver here's the most important sign of them all, ONE WAY, this WAY promises you Eternal Life with the Father."**

# SCARED TO LET IT GO
## Philippians 3:13 (NIV)

*Brothers, I do not consider myself yet to have taken hold of it. But one thing I do: Forgetting what is behind and straining toward what is ahead,*

While we sit and muse time after time, the question often arises somewhere in the recesses of our mind, what has hindered me from moving from this place that I sit and ponder day after day? Many of us struggle with our history. You know the things from our past and sometimes even our present. In most cases, the matters have to do with unforgiveness, bitterness, anger, past failures, and sometimes those things or persons that we are holding hostage, have moved on, not even knowing that somewhere lurking in the back of our minds, we are holding onto matters that they are simply clueless about or may have even forgotten even existed. The bigger picture is this, the matter at hand has held up our progress. I was recently at a women's retreat and had the opportunity to learn about archery, well while excited for this new venture, when I approached my chance at shooting, for some reason I became afraid. The pro while teaching me said, you're in the right place, your position is perfect, just let it go. Well it was not easy after all, while looking at the target through the bow, with arrow in hand, I froze. After 3 attempts I turned to the pro and said, I am scared to let it go. For some reason I had in my mind that if I had let the arrow go, it would some how back fire in my face. With tear-filled eyes, I clearly heard the Lord say, *LET IT Go!*

Here's what the Lord revealed to me later on that week; because I was so caught off guard and began to cry over the fact that I knew that it was true, I needed to let it GO, I never released the arrow from the bow. Well the Father said you missed the target.

**Let it go so you will not miss your target, you will never know what power you have if you won't let it go! Fear sparks us to use muscles we never knew we had.**

**"Sometimes power only presents itself in the presence of FEAR."**

# NO PHONE RECEPTION
### Daniel 2:19 (NKJ)

*And then a secret was revealed to Daniel in a night vision.*
*So Daniel blessed the God of heaven.*

One weekend, a very dear friend of mine and I went away to a women's conference in the mountains of Idyllwild, California. Once I was settled in my cabin, it was my intent to call my husband and my children to tell them all about our drive on the way and possibly what the rest of this weekend may have in store for us. I opened my cell phone only to notice the phone screen clearly read "***NO SERVICE***." Well, you have to know that all of the 25 or so other women were all in the same position. However, one of the other ladies said, "If you stand by this pole at this odd angle, you may just be in luck."

Well rested and satisfied from the fellowship we had the night before, we ladies decided that later on that day we would go *UP to* the prayer mountain and pray. It should be no shock to know that most of us still had our phones on our person, even though we had no service.

After being at the feet of Jesus on the mountain and taking in all that God's great canvas had for us, in the silence, I heard a beep from my phone indicating that I had voicemails and text messages. But, how could this be? The higher we went up, the better the reception. We not only had a signal to dial, but we were able to receive text messages. I was then able to make the call that the night before which was impossible to make with no connection delays. While my family was happy to hear from me, I was grateful for the revelation.

**"The higher we go, the better the reception."**

# ON TIME

### Ecclesiastes 3:1 (KJV)

*To everything there is a season, and a time to every purpose
under the heaven:*

The waiting is the hardest part of a promise. Often times we find ourselves waiting, waiting and more waiting. Look at it through the eyes of a child whom you promised a new toy on payday and that day is 12 days from now, or you say when the weather gets warmer, then we can do Disneyland, but each day after that get's even colder than the day you made the promise. Well my friend so goes the law of the job you have, the paydays have been set. We have no control over the seasons either; they have been set and go as follows; Winter, Spring, Summer and Fall. This order was set before the foundations of the world were formed and so is the seasons of our life. The word of encouragement is this, hold on to the promise for your coming season. It may come in Winter, maybe Spring, could be Summer, your time is coming maybe even in the Fall. However, trust it's coming, how do I know? Because I know the promise keeper, for HE is not only the promise keeper, but hear this, He is also the season maker and if the seasons know when their time has come, so should we because HE always keeps HIS word.

**The ability to accept and appreciate God's perfect timing,
is a choice, and when you do, here's your opportunity, to
discover real peace in the promise, and what a promise it is.**

**"The promise is LIFE eternal
with the maker of Heaven and Earth."**

# VICTORY IS

## Philippians 3:12 (MSG)

*I am not saying that I have this all together, that I have it made. However, I am well on my way, reaching out for Christ, who has so wondrously reached out for me. Friends, do not get me wrong: By no means do I count myself an expert in all of this, but I've got my eye on the goal, where God is beckoning us onward—to Jesus. I'm off and running, and I'm not turning back.*

In the above-mentioned text, Paul is stating, that he runs after the ONE who has already apprehended him.

Celebration grants us an overwhelming sense of I can, and I have just done the impossible by maintaining my course in the process of what may appear to be an obstacle. Therefore, once I have obtained, I stick to my course and maintain the truth, which holds the promise. His promises are yes and amen. What makes this obtainable? By simply asking the One who knows the path that HE, before the foundations of the world were formed, created with my very life in mind? Now knowing the truth that I shall forever hold dear in my heart, that I am a work in progress, I run daily after the ONE who has already apprehended me. No one knows when the hour will come, but it shall, and on that day, we together will rejoice over our triumphal victory!

## Victory
**Triumph, success, mastery, award, prize, conquest celebrate; jubilee, ovation, rejoicing, VICTORY**

### "Time to celebrate our <u>VICTORY!</u>"

# MUST STAY FOCUSED

## Matthew 7:13-14 (NKJV)

*"Enter by the narrow gate; for wide is the gate and broad is the way that leads to destruction, and there are many who go in by it. Because narrow is the gate and difficult is the way which leads to life, and there are few who find it."*

Narrow denotes that it's the only way to live eternally with God. Another way of saying it is, not going to be easy, in fact it might just be hard, slender, tight, and for many just down right difficult, never the less, all the words mean the same thing, it almost feels impossible to achieve. Then there are those of us that will say, if I could just focus then maybe, no not even a maybe, if I focus then the road may not seem as narrow, slender, tight, close  or as hard. When I focus on what's in store, it's not going to be easy but it is according to the Word, the only way. For God came in the flesh and died for us, so His purpose is good for us because he again, made a way for us to get back to Him. Focus!!!

**"Getting to Heaven will be a narrow road, so I must stay *FOCUSED*."**

## CHAPTER THREE

# FORGIVENESS

## Colossians 3:13 (AB)

*Be gentle and forbearing with one another and, if one has a difference (a grievance or complaint) against another, readily pardoning each other; even as the Lord has [freely] forgiven you, so must you also [forgive].*

FORGIVING VS. FORGETTING

JUSTIFIED

GRACE FOR GRACE

A CLEAN BREAK

TIS ONLY BY

MY ALABASTER BOX

HE CHOSE HIS INFORMANT

# FORGIVING VS. FORGETTING

## Mark 11:26 (NKJV)

*But if ye do not forgive, neither will your Father which is in heaven forgive your trespasses.*

When someone has hurt you, I mean really hurt you; it's no easy way to let it go. The strange thing is that if you ask for a natural way to heal, there is no simple solution to the matter of your heart, why? Because the key word here is your heart. Just like a product bought at an appliance store, they generally come with a manual to let you know about the upkeep of the appliance, or how to trouble shoot any problems. In fact, you can call the manufacturer. So does this apply when it comes to maker of your very heart? HE knows how extensive the work needed is, to get it to properly function in order for it to complete its needed course. Some may say it's the forgiving that is easy, and that the forgetting is the harder of the two, I beg to differ.

Forgiving from my standards is like letting the offender get away with their offense, and the forgetting makes you believe it never happened. Both are the furthest thing from the truth. Forgiving is for you, the offended, so that you are not held hostage to the pain. Forgetting, why would you try? It is the hurt that brought growth to an area of your life that you did not know existed until a hurt exposed it. Case in point; JESUS has visible scars to remind HIM of what HE did for us, and this being the reason that HE intercedes for us. The scars are a reminder of what HE endured for us on the cross. Can you imagine for a moment, if HE ceased praying to Himself on our behalf, the pain would be just that pain? Do you want to see the real glory in forgiveness? Freedom for you, trust in the FATHER that HE will heal it, and redemption to the offender. Christ wants us to be more like HIM in all things, and another way of saying redemption is ransom. Is that not what CHRIST did for us? HE paid a ransom for our very lives, so why should we not do the same for our offender? The joy of the One, who understands freedom, is a joy we should all seek after. It is found in FORGIVENESS.

**"I would rather live my days knowing forgiveness, and remember that I don't have to forget than to live in bondage."**

# JUSTIFIED

## Galatians 3:24 (NKJV)

*Therefore the law was our tutor to bring us to Christ,*
*that we might be justified by faith.*

If this point of scripture does not shout from the mountains I am not sure what else needs to be said. Get it, I mean really get it because we were born into sin. God himself sent a tutor to instruct us until we found our way to Him. Now I don't know about you, but what case do you know of that the Judge would send a teacher to lead, govern and guide you till you made it right, just to hear the gavel go down to say justified/cleared, and you know you were guilty as SIN for the crime the DA (devils advocate) charged you with. The Heavenly Father thought it more urgent, that His loyalty (faith) take a plea of not guilty to bring us to Christ through justified blood.

**"Our Justification is granted because of the tutor and the Blood that hit the mercy seat."**

# GRACE FOR GRACE

## 2 Corinthians 12:9 (KJV)

*And he said unto me, My grace is sufficient for thee: for my strength is made perfect in weakness. Most gladly therefore will I rather glory in my infirmities, that the power of Christ may rest upon me.*

The grace I gave as the Christ, you shall also give. If I decided to say I can't take the cup, or the pain was too intense so I threw in the towel and I was innocent, then look closely at what I did on the cross! I gave you the grace you did not deserve and as LORD, I am asking that you do the same.

The grace of GOD is our source of salvation. Just as HE so freely gave to us, we should freely extend one to another, there is nothing we can do to change HIS saving plan for us.

Grace for Grace. It is sufficient for our times of weakness.

**"The same Grace I gave, you must give to one another."**

# A CLEAN BREAK

## Ephesians 4:30-32 (MSG)

*Don't grieve God. Don't break his heart. His Holy Spirit, moving and breathing in you, is the most intimate part of your life, making you fit for himself. Don't take such a gift for granted.*

*Make a clean break with all cutting, backbiting, profane talk. Be gentle with one another, sensitive. Forgive one another as quickly and thoroughly as God in Christ forgave you.*

Who would want to be responsible for breaking the Master's heart? I believe with every ounce of my being, that God loves us more than we will ever be able to comprehend. Think about it, if you had the option to write your owner's manual, explain how to be loved, how to reverence, how to be taken care of properly, would you? Seriously, this is what it would look like…..Perfect peace. Why then have we been so lazy, and quick to forget that each time we allow sin to rule for even a moment, we have just grieved God? For this reason did I mention earlier, that God so loves us, it is really hard to fathom because he not only gave us a blueprint, along with this, He also gives us grace and mercy. In other words, room to get on His good side. Deliberate with yourself for a second, or how ever long it takes you to grasp what it is about Sin, that you would rather have it, than God.

**"A Clean Break, letting go of anything that will make Dad weep."**

**"A Clean Break, Forgiving quickly, often and thoroughly."**

# TIS ONLY BY

### Ephesians 2:8 (AB)

*For it is by free grace (God's unmerited favor) that you are saved (delivered from judgment and made partakers of Christ's salvation) through [your] faith. And this [salvation] is not of yourselves [of your own doing, it came not through your own striving], but it is the gift of God.*

The grace of God is our ultimate source of our salvation; however, faith is the channel by which we accept this amazing gift. Therefore, none of us can walk around and say we did this thing called life all on our own. Jesus' blood is the only reason we can even approach the Father. If it had not been for Jesus who was on our side, our enemy would have swallowed us up (Psalm 124:1).

But, God in His infinite mercy said NO. Can you imagine your life with no grace attached to it? What a chilling image? Life without it would be very horrifying. Think of it this way, your sin issue and you only have 3 chances to get it right, the earth would be empty, there would be no you or me. Here's where we can shout. God knew our struggle before the earth was even formed, so HE imparted grace as part of our journey to get us back to Him. What is grace? It is favor, a pardon, His love and compassion for us; it is His ultimate kindness toward us given daily.

Our struggle has Grace attached to it, with a guarantee that we can trust, will get us back to the Master. However, the key is this, Christ died once for this purpose; you should not play around with your limited grace, for it too, has an expiration date.

G ~ Generous
R ~ Relief
A ~ Acquitted
C ~ Clemency
E ~ Exonerate

# MY ALABASTER BOX

## Luke 7:41-50 (NIV)

*Two men owed money to a certain moneylender. One owed him five hundred
denarii,[1] and the other fifty. Neither of them had the money to pay him back,
so he canceled the debts of both. Now which of them will love him more?"*

*Simon replied, "I suppose the one who had the bigger debt canceled."
"You have judged correctly," Jesus said.*

*Then he turned toward the woman and said to Simon, "Do you see this
woman? I came into your house. You did not give me any water for my feet,
but she wet my feet with her tears and wiped them with her hair. You did not
give me a kiss, but this woman, from the time I entered, has not stopped kiss-
ing my feet. You did not put oil on my head, but she has poured perfume on
my feet. Therefore, I tell you, her many sins have been forgiven—for she loved
much. But he who has been forgiven little loves little."*

*Then Jesus said to her, "Your sins are forgiven."*

*The other guests began to say among themselves,
"Who is this who even forgives sins?"*

*Jesus said to the woman, "Your faith has saved you; go in peace."*

Jesus, Thank you for letting me cry at your feet, and when I did,
you forgave me. You knew all about me when I came, and you still
offered your Blood to save my sinful life, so that I may **live**….

When we said yes to your gift of life, we brought our Alabaster
Boxes to you, and we poured the precious oil of worship at your feet.

### "None of US has the same Alabaster Box."

# HE CHOSE HIS INFORMANT

## Mark 3:13-15 &19 (NKJV)

*He went up on the mountain and called to Him those He Himself wanted.*
*And they came to Him. Then He appointed twelve, that they might be with*
*Him and that He might send them out to preach, to have power to heal*
*sicknesses, and to cast out demons.*
*And Judas Iscariot, who also betrayed Him, And they went into a house.*

Thief, greedy, betrayer, suicidal, double-crosser, uncommitted pretender, one cheek kisser, and the informant, chosen by Christ to fulfill the path that would lead Him to the cross. Judas Iscariot, we have heard his name over a course of study, some of us have read the very text, and yet we still ask the same question repeatedly, why did HE select him? The answer, unpretentious but quaint, is to fulfill the destiny of the cross. I saw a T-shirt once that read," Every Crew has one." On it was a picture of a rat. The irony here is, Jesus knew who, and when. The Word tells us that, He will not have us ignorant to the enemy's devices **2Corinthians 2:11**, Jesus, having knowledge of what Judas was going to do, proves this promise. Jesus told the others, "the hour has come; behold the Son of Man is being betrayed into the hands of sinners. Let us be going. My betrayer is at hand." The FBI and CIA have been known to use informants to accomplish a big job, but in these cases, if the informant is identified, he/she has the opportunity to go into a witness protection program, to keep safe from the enemy that they brought down. I would like to propose to you, that because of Jesus' death, death, hell and the grave were defeated. Judas was identified by the multitudes, as the informant of the Savior. However, what Christ had accomplished at the cross, Judas, having taken his own life, was unable to taste the grace or mercy that Jesus freely gave the rest of us. In fact, Judas was caught by the enemy that actually set him up, to betray the One he walked with, whom he saw do, the very things that Jesus said was the reason He called the 12. A careful note to take here is this, Judas was not around long enough to know Revelation 12:11 that clearly states, "We overcome, by the blood of the Lamb and our testimony," which means Calvary's purpose took the responsibility of the testimony he could have had, had he not let his own guilt cause him to take his life.

**Mark confirms this witness protection program when it states:**
**Even for the betraycr forgiveness was prepared.**

## CHAPTER FOUR

# FAITH

## Hebrews 11:6 (ESV)

*And without faith it is impossible to please Him, for whoever would draw near to God must believe that he exists and that He rewards those who seek Him.*

ASK HIM EVERYTHING

NOT GUILTY

NO TRESPASSING

LYING OUT OF FEAR

STOP LEANING

CHANGE WILL GET YOU IN

NO AUTO-PILOT NEEDED

ROADSIDE ASSISTANCE

NO PEEKING

LET THEM SING

THE SHADOW WILL DO

HAND IN THE DARK

WORK IT

# ASK HIM EVERYTHING

## Luke 11:10 (NIV)

*For everyone who asks receives; he who seeks finds; and to him who knocks, the door will be opened.*

I was told along time ago that the only stupid question is the one not asked. Though this text is not referring to it initially, it opens up a stream of loaded opportunities with the One who knows what we will ever  have need of even before we ask to ensure we make our way in this life. I have found that pride has no place in the life of a Christian, we cannot be so proud that we do not ask for the things that we need.

### Ask:
To beg, solicit, implore, petition, beseech, supplication, request, entreat, and request.

### Philippians 4:6 (NIV)
*Do not be anxious about anything, but in everything, by prayer and petition, with thanksgiving, present your requests to God.*

**"Ask and it shall be given, request and it shall be granted."**

# NOT GUILTY

## Revelation 12:10 (NKJV)

*Then I heard a loud voice saying in heaven, "Now salvation, and strength, and the kingdom of our God, and the power of His Christ have come, for the accuser of our brethren, who accused them before our God day and night, has been cast down."*

Satan is styled the "accuser of the brethren" (Rev. 12:10), as seeking to uphold his influence among men, by bringing false charges against Christians, with the view of weakening their influence and injuring the cause by which they are identified. The Jews regarded him as the "*accuser*" of men before God, laying to their charge the violations of the law of which they were guilty, and demanding their punishment. The same Greek word, rendered "*accuser*," found in John 8:1 brings a charge against another.

Remember when you were told, "be careful what you say about others, as well as every time you point your finger at someone there are three pointing back at you." The accuser knows what he is doing and we often let him use us to assist him in his tactics. The text above is clear, he is tattle telling on us day and night reporting all our mistakes to set us up to look like failures. Be encouraged, it is not a secret that JESUS said that HE is praying for us that our faith will not fail.(**Luke 22:31-32**) My advice to you is this; walk carefully, pray without ceasing, stay in the Word, and stop giving him a reason to tattle on you any longer. The phrase "Not Guilty" applies to us, because we have been forgiven, by the One true Judge.

**"Stop playing with an enemy that likes to tattle."**

# NO TRESPASSING

## 2 Chronicles 30:7 (KJV)

*And be not ye like your fathers, and like your brethren, which trespassed against the LORD God of their fathers, who therefore gave them up to desolation, as ye see.*

When we put our matters in the hand of God, we are to leave them there. If we do not, we are in violation, for we are treading on illegal territory and can be arrested. Because just as the sign says, violators will be prosecuted, and fined to the full extent of the law. The subject matter is clear, we put our issues in the hand of the Judge of the universe, and let's say we will not go back and touch it, but we often do, and when we do, it is like stealing from HIM as if He couldn't fix the matter without the assistance or the counsel of Me, Myself, and I, Attorney at Law, Esq.

## Job 15:8-9 (AB)

*Were you present to hear the secret counsel of God? What do you know that we do not know? What do you understand that is not equally clear to us?*

### Fix:
To mend, establish, repair, stabilize, adjust, settle, decide, place, fasten, prepare.

I am foolish enough to believe that the God we serve can do just that FIX it. Therefore, we need not be in violation.

**Why be arrested for foolish matters....no trespassing.**
**Trespassing is a risk we should not consider.**

# LYING OUT OF FEAR

## Genesis 12:10-13(MSG)

*Then a famine came to the land. Abram went down to Egypt to live; it was a hard famine. As he drew near to Egypt, he said to his wife, Sarai, "Look, we both know that you're a beautiful woman, when the Egyptians see you they're going to say, 'Aha! That's his wife' and kill me, but they'll let you live! Do me a favor; tell them you're    my sister. Because of you, they'll welcome me and let me live."*

We are all guilty of it at some point in our lives, or maybe you have not ever been so desperate that the easy way out was a simple little lie. Well if you have never been there you can skip this one all together, but remember no one is reading this but you, so don't lie to yourself, to be honest, that's generally where the lie starts. The problem here, is that we often lie when we think we need to save our own hide.The other issue is that we have to try and remember the story (lie) we told. Oh you say, "I don't lie ever," but we often find ourselves lying when we think it will save some one's feelings, or ladies we don't tell our spouses how much money we really spent. This one should make us all laugh, when someone ask your weight or what size we wear, do you tell them the truth? Well if your answer was no, then it is a lie and to whom do we owe an apology, none other than GOD himself. In the scripture text noted above, Abram ask Sarai to lie so that Pharaoh would not take her into his harem that he may live. Not trusting God was his issue even though God's faithfulness had already been proven time and time again. So the next time you are faced with saving your own hide, take note of this, your hide was already saved and you did not have to lie for it, in fact, because HE knew you would is why he did it anyway.

**"No need to lie, but in fact just trust in the ONE who sent you."**

# STOP LEANING

## Proverbs 3:5-6(NIV)

*Trust in the Lord with all your heart and lean not unto your own understanding. In all your ways acknowledge him and he will make your paths straight.*

**Joshua 1:8** says, this book of law shall not depart from your mouth; but you shall meditate in it day and night, that you may observe to do according to all that is written in it, for then you will make your way prosperous, and then you will have good success. For have I not said, be strong and courageous; do not be afraid, nor be dismayed for the Lord your God is with you wherever you go.

If possible we really need to stop, look, and listen to what the Lord is saying to us, HE  makes it clear and the bottom line is this…… ……I've got it all figured out for you, from the start, all the way to the finish…so let's just go on this planned journey together. The blueprints already on paper, which can not be erased, along with the navigation set by ME, for your journey.

**"Use the blueprints and follow the navigation."**

# CHANGE WILL GET YOU IN

### Matthew 18:3(NIV)

*And he said: "I tell you the truth, unless you change and become like little children, you will never enter the kingdom of heaven.*

There is no other way for us to enter into the Kingdom, lest we change. Like a child we must be, because they have faith that we will do what we say, we must be the same in our walk with Christ. We must believe that His promises are yes and amen. We must know that apart from Him we are nothing. We must know with every fiber of our being that He really did pay it all at the cross. We must believe that the Blood is real and that its purpose is to give us the life HE predetermined from the start of this thing called life.

**The only way to survive is CHANGE~**

# NO AUTO PILOT NEEDED

## John 14:26-27 (NKJV)

*"But the Helper, the Holy Spirit, whom the Father will send in My name, He will teach you all things, and bring to your remembrance all things that I said to you. Peace I leave with you, My peace I give to you; not as the world gives do I give to you. Let not your heart be troubled, neither let it be afraid."*

The Holy Spirit/Comforter plants truth in our minds, convince us of God's will for our lives, and remind us when we stray away from it. The auto pilot is a system often used by the pilot and crew to fly the plane once it's reach the designated altitude and flight path. This system allows the pilot to rest when tired and not have to actively engage the controls. However, the pilot must use his/her skill and training for takeoff and landing of the vessel. These are two of the most important parts of the flight, the beginning and the end. Can we then liken the Holy Spirit/Comforter if you will, to a pilot who never needs to use the auto pilot system, because the Holy Spirit **never** sleeps nor slumber? So let's sit back, trust God, and allow the Holy Spirit to control the paths of our lives, because He is the Alpha and Omega. The Beginning and the End!!

The amazing thing about the auto pilot is that before it can go on any journey it has to be set to ensure it will accomplish what it has been set out to do. So there is no need to worry, you will get to your predestined end, because

**The Holy Spirit/Comforter goes before you always. Just be certain to ask HIM to come along.**

# ROADSIDE ASSISTANCE

### Psalms 91:11~Matthew 4:6~Luke 4:10

## Psalm 91:11-12 (NKJV)

*For He shall give His angels charge over you,*
*To keep you in all your ways.*
*In their hands they shall bear you up,*
*Lest you dash your foot against a stone.*

## Matthew 4:6 (KJV)

*And saith unto him, If thou be the Son of God, cast thyself down: for it is*
*written, He shall give his angels charge concerning thee: and in their hands*
*they shall bear thee up, lest at any time thou dash thy foot against a stone.*

## Luke 4:10 (Today's New International Version)

*For it is written:*
*'He will command his angels concerning you*
*to guard you carefully;*

The Father will protect us no matter the danger. On a dark isolated road, the greatest confidence we can have is knowing that if we do not have AAA we have great roadside assistance, called RAA-roadside assistance angels.

Whether it is a flat tire, out of gas, a fender bender, or a cracked windshield, no need to panic, your roadside assistance is on their job until your natural help arrives.

### Your policy number is P9111M46L410

# NO PEEKING
## "No sneak previews for this life"

### 1 Corinthians 2:9 (KJV)

*But, as it is written, Eye hath not seen, nor ear heard, neither have entered into the heart of man, the things which God hath prepared for them that love Him.*

Life sometimes throws us a curve ball, and in most cases, many of us are not prepared for it. Because it took us by surprise, we begin to think we did something wrong, or that maybe we some how did not hear God, and clearly we made a major mistake in how we got where we are. Some examples I chose to use are common life choices we make everyday; our mates, the college we chose for our higher learning, the sports we put our kids in, the house we purchased, or even the car we decided on. The ironic thing is the moment an issue presents itself, panic of the mind begins. Our spouse fails us, no degree in hand; your child breaks an arm, the house floods, or the car, repossessed. These are those moments where we neglect our knowledge that <u>all</u> things work together for our good. The truth of the matter is this known fact, if God gave us a sneak preview of every aspect of our life, including our failures, our growth would be stagnant to say the least... There are many things we forget when a trial hits, we start to question our very wisdom that God so freely gave to us by way of His word, such as; many are the plans of man but it is the Lord's plan that will always prevail. Ask yourself this, if the Lord gave you the chance for PEEK-A-BOO, would you take it? This is a game for infants, or children. It also gives us a chance to see where our faith is, so if your answer is YES, then please  take notes, because if we were to take a peek, for many of us there would have never been a spouse, education, sports, no house, and many of us would be on a bus. It is for this reason, why there is no PEEKING and no sneak previews. Because the Father wants us to know that though things may come that catch us by surprise, He is always on top of what is coming, the big and small matters. He is involved.

**"Peek-a-boo is a game for infants & toddlers, grow up."**

# LET THEM SING

## Matthew 6:26 (NKJV)

*Look at the birds of the air, for they neither sow nor reap nor gather into
barns; yet your heavenly Father feeds them.
Are you not of more value than they?*

Have you ever watched the birds in the early morning of Spring? It is a sight to see as well as music to your very ears. I became fascinated with birds as a young girl, they look as though they have not a care in the world, well what do they have to be concerned about? They literally fly by faith! So they fill their lungs and sing, they do what they were called to do. Their worship to God is the song they sing as a way of saying Thank You for keeping your promise. The Word says that HE takes care of them in such a way, that they do not worry about what they will eat or where they will live. They understand Gods order. While the male bird is building the nest, the female bird goes out nearby, where she is able to hear her song of thanks to him as well as to God. The Word says to give honor where honor is due, and because she flies by faith, as well as understands order, she sings. Therefore, she works to utilize her gift as he uses his. Thus not sitting on her gift and nor is he.

**"Why worry just use your gifts."**

# THE SHADOW WILL DO

### Acts 5:15-16(NIV)

*As a result, people brought the sick into the streets and laid them on beds and mats so that at least Peter's <u>shadow</u> might fall on some of them as he passed by. Crowds gathered also from the towns around Jerusalem, bringing their sick and those tormented by evil spirits, and all of were healed.*

**Shadow:**
A reflected image, shelter from danger or observation

If we could truly get a full understanding of the power of the Holy Spirit, how much more would we let go and let God? The mere fact that people came from everywhere not expecting to be spoken to, or even touched is astounding! They had enough faith in what the cross had accomplished, so they came and prayed that they could somehow get in the way of Peter's shadow and be healed of their ills. So I must ask you this, what affect would your shadow have on those needing a healing? The knowledge here is that the Holy Spirit that was present there was the dubious power present when Jesus Christ was raised from the grave. Well that same powerful presence that was there is here for us. Meditate here just for a moment, think about what we have been left with from the Master, what power we have been trusted with, but what are we doing with it really? Have we established that what we have been given really is ours to use in the time of need? Not just for us, but for others, that when they witness this power activated through us, they desire to know the One that trusted us enough to give it to us as a gift.

**Ask yourself, are you walking in enough faith
to activate your shadow?**
***Because the shadow will do!***

# HAND IN THE DARK

### Psalm 139:10-12 (NKJV)

*Even there Your hand shall lead me,*
*and Your right hand shall hold me.*
*If I say, "Surely the darkness shall fall on me,"*
*Even the night shall be light about me;*
*Indeed, the darkness shall not hide from You,*
*but the night shines as the day;*
*the darkness and the light are both alike to You.*

God is omnipresent: He is present everywhere. What a relief to know that no matter where I am, God is there with me! Remember as a child you were afraid of the dark. Recently, I arose in the midnight hour to go get a glass of water, but never turned on a light to find my way until I reached my destination, the kitchen down stairs. Well from dark to light, then light to dark I stumbled only to find my wonderful husband's hand waiting to help me make it back to my resting place, I said "honey I can see your hand in the dark." What a revelation, God said, He is the same, and if I look closely I will find that His hand is there too in my darkness, in fact, God would turn the darkness to light just to find me. Because He opposes darkness, there is a guarantee I will not be in the dark long, in fact, the dark places light up when I reach for HIS hand.

### "I can see YOUR hand in the dark."

# WORK IT

## James 2:14 (KJV)

*What doth it profit, my brethren, though a man say he hath faith, and have not works? can faith save him?*

**Here's the Master's plan (blue print) of action for FAITH at work.**

### Ask-

**James 1:6** *But let him ask in faith, with no doubting, for he who doubts is like a wave of the sea driven and tossed by the wind.*

### Believe-

**Galatians 3:22** *But the Scripture has confined all under sin, that the promise by faith in Jesus Christ might be given to those who believe.*

### Confess-

**Romans 10:9** *That if thou shalt confess with thy mouth the Lord Jesus, and shalt believe in thine heart that God hath raised him from the dead, thou shalt be saved.*

### Know His Word-

**Isaiah 55:11** *So shall my word be that goeth forth out of my mouth: it shall not return unto me void, but it shall accomplish that which I please, and it shall prosper in the thing whereto I sent it.*

### Ask ~ Believe ~ Confess ~ His Word
### Demonstration-

**1 Corinthians 2:4** *And my speech and my preaching was not with enticing words of man's wisdom, but in demonstration of the Spirit and of power:*

### Expectation-

**Psalm 62:5** *My soul, wait thou only upon God; for my expectation is from him.*

### Give *HIM* Glory-

**Matthew 5:16** *Let your light so shine before men, that they may see your good works, and glorify your Father which is in heaven.*

### PRAISE

**Psalm 150:6** *Let every thing that hath breath praise the LORD. Praise ye the LORD.*

### Demonstrate ~ Expectation ~ Give Him Glory ~Praise

### Faith has a blue print~Work It

## CHAPTER FIVE

# WISDOM

## Proverbs 1:7 (KJV)

*The fear of the LORD is the beginning of knowledge: but fools despise wisdom and instruction.*

**THE INNER ME**

**MAGNIFY**

**WHAT A PRESENCE?**

**FLASHLIGHT OR LIGHTHOUSE**

**HIDDEN MYSTERIES**

**FLOAT**

**WHY BARTER?**

# THE INNER ME

## Psalm 119:33-36(MSG)

*God, teach me lessons for living so I can stay the course.*
*Give me insight so I can do what you tell me—*
*my whole life one long, obedient response.*
*Guide me down the road of your commandments;*
*I love traveling this freeway!  Give me a bent(desire)*
*for your words of wisdom,  and not for piling up loot.*

We all have the ability to succeed in all we desire, but, this can only be accomplished with God as our ultimate source.  We could be an excellent husband, wife, or friend; however it is the matters of the heart that keep us restricted.  Strongholds are real.  But at the end of the day, it's what we choose to do with those strongholds that matters—either they control us or we control them.

Yoda say's "Don't try, just do."   We are our own greatest enemy. It is the *inner me* that we fight.  The foolishness of the matter is this; there are some enemies (inner me) we should not dare fight alone. Father GOD has already provided a way for our escape—*grace and mercy.*  With these two benefactors comes a bodyguard, the Holy Ghost, who can and will fight what we can't. When CHRIST defeated hell, He proved that surely we can defeat our flesh, the matters of our heart.  Choose life, and when you do, *all* that you *will* to do, you will SUCCEED at being the best husband, wife or friend. For in this state is found a peace that surpasses all understanding.

**"Don't allow your Inner-me to be your greatest Enemy."**

# MAGNIFY

## Psalm 34:3-5 (NIV)

*Glorify the LORD with me;*
*let us exalt his name together.*

*I sought the LORD, and he answered me;*
*he delivered me from all my fears.*

*Those who look to him are radiant;*
*their faces are never covered with shame.*

### Magnify:
### Enlarge, intensify, and make bigger, increase

Ask yourselves, why is it that when a problem comes in our direction, we make it bigger than it really is? Don't get me wrong, there are troubles that can consume us, but is there anything too hard for God to handle? The Word tells us that what's in a man's heart proceeds from his mouth. So how can we combat this approach? Magnify HIM instead. Think about it, you focus your energy on the Master instead of your cross; can you imagine what joy this would bring to the Father? You see, when we put Him above the ordeal, it shows a form of great reverence and it witness to those around us, because there is something to be said about how we respond to life's circumstances and you never know who's watching, learning and praying. In fact, I say it this way; my blessings are predicated on my response. When I murmur and complain, I think I slow God down. Here's a task worth entertaining, ask your Lord what's the lesson in this trial? Ask Him to show you how to respond, so that when it's all said and done, there is really NO SHAME, and that with great dignity, I tell about the test I passed, that today is my TESTIMONY!

### "I choose to MAGNIFY the ONE
### who can make my burdens <u>small</u>."

# WHAT A PRESENCE

### Luke 1:41(MSG)

*When Elizabeth heard Mary's greeting, the baby in her womb leaped. She*
*was filled with the Holy Spirit, and sang out exuberantly,*
*you're so blessed among women,*
*and the babe in your womb, also blessed!*
*And why am I so blessed that*
*the mother of my Lord visits me?*
*The moment the sound of your*
*greeting entered my ears,*
*The babe in my womb*
*skipped like a lamb for sheer joy.*

**"His very presence should cause us to leap**
**when we are in HIS presence."**

# FLASHLIGHT OR LIGHTHOUSE

### Psalms 119:105(KJV)

*Thy word is a lamp unto my feet, And a light to my path.*

Imagine understanding the authority that we absolutely have in Christ, and knowing that when HE is present, which is constant, how we'd approach most, if not all of life's storms. Many would venture to say that unless you were in the storm with me or were a witness to it, you have no clue. Well you are probably correct, but I am not saying don't panic, but I am stating that if you know the One that has all power to cease the storm, why not simply say, Father I did not bring my flashlight on board, because I knew that it would be of no use to me or to the others watching in this dark and dim place in the middle of this sea and turbulence, but that in fact, you were ever present, and therefore like you did for Shadrach, Mishack, and Abendego, that you would be here in the midst of the fire with me, even as you were for Peter on the water, you could reach out and bring me into safety, as does the beacon light that the ships at sea need for guidance, and Father, you are for me;  My Lighthouse.

**"Why use a flashlight when I have the lighthouse."**

# HIDDEN MYSTERIES
## No eye ~ No Ear ~No Mind
### 1 Corinthians 2:6-9(NIV)

*We do, however, speak a message of wisdom among the mature, but not the wisdom of this age or of the rulers of this age, who are coming to nothing. No, we speak of God's secret wisdom, a wisdom that has been hidden and that God destined for our glory before time began. None of the rulers of this age understood it, for if they had, they would not have crucified the Lord of glory. However, as it is written:*
*No eye has seen, no ear has heard, no mind has conceived what God has prepared for those who love him* [10]*but God has revealed it to us by his Spirit. The Spirit searches all things, even the deep things of God.* [11]*For who among men knows the thoughts of a man except the man's spirit within him? In the same way no one knows the thoughts of God except the Spirit of God.* [12]*We have not received the spirit of the world but the Spirit who is from God, that we may understand what God has freely given us.* [13]*This is what we speak, not in words taught us by human wisdom but in words taught by the Spirit, expressing spiritual truths in spiritual words.*

Wisdom of the Word is not conceived because of book knowledge, but because our Father in heaven decided to impart revelation to us, to ensure we make positive and consistent choices, so that in all things HE will get the glory and the people of God whom He chose will follow. You see there is so much more working here by way of the Holy Spirit. The Holy Spirit is the creative side of God. In other words, He has the ability to teach us what no man or book ever could, think about it, the very first time you ever tried to read the Bible, if like most of us, it read like black book babble. But then one day, our Gracious Lord, Father, God, Savoir, our ransom, decided to let you and me in on the mysteries, the hidden parts, the secret Wisdom.

**"The Secret Wisdom, The hidden Mysteries Freely given From the Heart of the Manufacturer/Producer."**

# FLOAT

### Hebrews 12:1-2 (AB)

*THEREFORE THEN, since we are surrounded by so great a cloud of witnesses [who have borne testimony to the Truth], let us strip off and throw aside every encumbrance (unnecessary weight) and that sin which so readily (deftly and cleverly) clings to and entangles us, and let us run with patient endurance and steady and active persistence the appointed course of the race that is set before us,*
*Looking away [from all that will distract] to Jesus, Who is the Leader and the Source of our faith [giving the first incentive for our belief] and is also it's Finisher [bringing it to maturity and perfection]. He, for the joy [of obtaining the prize] that was set before Him, endured the cross, despising and ignoring the shame, and is now seated at the right hand of the throne of God.*

### Float:
To drift or be suspended on water or linger in space; to move easily or lightly; an exhibit in a parade or show.

Weight is everything that hinders us as believers/or runners. The only time a runner really needs weights, is when they are in training because it is then and only then that they need to know their own endurance and stamina. Once the training camp is over and the needed muscle is in place, the extra weights are just that, extra, which means more of a burden then any help at all. In order for us to move forward in the training camp, we need to acknowledge when we no longer need the weights. Christ has already done everything needed for us to endure in our faith. His mind was not on the agony or pain (Weight) of the cross, but on the souls that would be saved after his work was finished in boot camp, the work He did for us. Ride it out that's what it means to float.

So can we say it this way, that there are times when we may just need to linger?  In other words, just hold on (daydream), and then there will be times we just need to walk gingerly **(light)** and then other times when we may just have to be on display for the show, you know the parade. Did I mention who the grand marshal is of this great parade?  Something to consider is this, at the end of a parade the queen gets her crown. But not before she has taken the test, to ensure she can teach those that will need her advice as to how she was able to receive her crown.  The answer, simple… *While floating she still needed to add power to get there…*Trying to float with weights, impossible....too heavy, and it goes against the law=***Gravity.***

**Sometimes floating is necessary it requires no weights lest you could only go so far.**

# WHY BARTER

### Genesis 38:15-24 (MSG)

*Judah saw her and assumed she was a prostitute since she had veiled her face.
He left the road and went over to her. He said, "Let me sleep with you." He
had no idea that she was his daughter-in-law.*

*She said, "What will you pay me?"*

*"I'll send you," he said, "a kid goat from the flock."*

*She said, "Not unless you give me a pledge until you send it."*

*"So what would you want in the way of a pledge?"*

*She said, "Your personal seal-and-cord and the staff you carry."*

*He handed them over to her and slept with her. And she got pregnant.
She then left and went home. She removed her veil and put her widow's
clothes back on.*

*Judah sent the kid goat by his friend from Adullam to recover the pledge
from the woman. But he couldn't find her. He asked the men of that place,
"Where's the prostitute that used to sit by the road here near Enaim?"*

*They said, "There's never been a prostitute here."*

*He went back to Judah and said, "I couldn't find her. The men there said there
never has been a prostitute there."*

*Judah said, "Let her have it then. If we keep looking, everyone will be poking
fun at us. I kept my part of the bargain—I sent the kid goat but you couldn't
find her."*

*Three months or so later, Judah was told, "Your daughter-in-law has been
playing the whore—and now she's a pregnant whore."*

*Judah yelled, "Get her out here. Burn her up!"*

### Barter:

**Trade, sell out, sale, cheapen, close out, exchange, deal, bargain
negotiate, transfer goods over, to give and take, bid, haggle,
agreement, and contract.**

**" Why barter ? Instead pay the full price and reap the absolute
blessing & purpose."**

## CHAPTER SIX

# PRAISE

## Psalm 34:1 (KJV)

*I will bless the LORD at all times: his praise shall continually be in my mouth.*

PRAISE TO LIVE

POWER AND PURPOSE OF PRAISE

PRAISE AN EXECUTED ACTION

PRAISE FREQUENCY

REASONS FOR PRAISE

WHAT KEEPS US FROM IT

MADE FOR THIS

# NO PRESERVATIVES

## John 6:53 (MSG)

*But Jesus didn't give an inch. "Only insofar as you eat and drink flesh and
blood, the flesh and blood of the Son of Man, do you have life within you.
The one who brings a hearty appetite to this eating and drinking has eternal
life and will be fit and ready for the Final Day. My flesh is real food and my
blood is real drink. By eating my flesh and drinking my blood, you enter into
me and I into you. In the same way that the fully alive Father sent me here
and I live because of him, so the one who makes a meal of me lives because of
me. This is the Bread from heaven. Your ancestors ate bread and later died.
Whoever eats this Bread will live always."*

**<u>Preservative:</u>
Something that preserves or has the power of preserving; an
additive used to protect against decay, discoloration,
or spoilage.**

The times we are in, are all about image, in which exercise
and the foods we eat play a pivotal role in how we approach
our everyday activities. We read the labels on the foods we
purchase and most of us are always on a scale (not me). Well I
do watch what I eat, but if it is loaded with sugar, high in fat,
has MSG, or preservatives, it will not be on my plate or even
in my pantry, just ask Chelsea or Jaylon. Why, because it has
been proven that these things are not good for the heart. So
then, why when it comes to our spiritual life, do we take for
granted that the food we consume for our natural well-being
is the same for our spiritual food supply?  The blood has accomplished what it was suppose to do. There are no extra
additives, you cannot dilute it, and no cleanser that can get
this stain out, it will forever meet the purpose of the Cross.

We say the blood of Jesus covers, but we do not act, live or respond as if we know it to be true. In recent years, everyone has come to know that the best food is the organic foods, but yes my healthy friend it is going to cost you.

**The Word of GOD is the food that has no preservatives**
**Eat it daily,**
**Exercise it daily**
**Digest it daily,**
**Drink your 8oz daily**
**"This will make your Heart healthy all your days for**
**the eternal life you are promised."**

# THE FRAMED PHOTO

### Proverbs 14:30 (CEV)

*It's healthy to be content, but envy can eat you up.*

Isn't it ironic how we are all guilty in some shape form or fashion, of looking at someone else's life/photo, and some kind of way putting ourselves in the framed photo? The reason I say ironic is because it truly is just that. The reality is this; you & I do not know how many shots it took to get that perfect shot. How long did it take them to get the red eyes out, the color just right? Everyone sitting still all at the same time, the picture may be blurry, color off, someone blinked so we start over...... or maybe the photographer wanted it to be black and white, now that's funny, no one ever wants it black & white anymore because that's the naked truth, the truth of how we captured what use to be and made it for us today. Some of us, if we are honest, just settle for the sepia color, why? Because it resembles antique, well the problem with this is antique implies used before, and again we do not want what someone else has already used. We should want only what was made for us. Take your own picture my friend, buy your own frame, then when others see it, you can tell them the story that goes along with it...

**Do not envy my photo, it was more work than you can see, but the frame has helped it to look like the Masterpiece that it was destined to be. It cost much more than the price tag that it was labeled with, in fact it cost the Son of God His life...Priceless.**

# PRAISE TO LIVE

## Psalm 119:175(NKJV)

*Let me live that I may Praise you, and may your law sustain me.*

The only way we can make it in this hell bent world, is if He will keep our days in His hands and allow us every chance to come to Him with Praise consistently on our lips. Is there anyone under the skies to compare this awesome God to? Do we really need an explanation why praise is essential? One answer is apparent, it produces POWER. For once, wouldn't you like to see that tormenting struggle knocked to its face and the arms of your offender drop at his side? Well I have come today tell you how to get it done. Lift your voice, shout out to God in triumph, and sing a praise of Victory. If you are reading this you have breath, if you have breath, let the Praise begin!

"Breathing indicates living, the directive clear"

### Psalm 150:6 (NKJV)
*Let everything that has BREATH praise the LORD. Praise ye the Lord.*

# POWER AND PURPOSE OF PRAISE

### Acts 16:25-30 (NKJV)

But at midnight Paul and Silas were praying and singing hymns to God, and the prisoners were listening to them. Suddenly there was a great earthquake, so that the foundations of the prison were shaken; and immediately all the doors were opened and everyone's chains were loosed. And the keeper of the prison, awaking from sleep and seeing the prison doors open, supposing the prisoners had fled, drew his sword and was about to kill himself. But Paul called with a loud voice, saying, "Do yourself no harm, for we are all here." Then he called for a light, ran in, and fell down trembling before Paul and Silas. And he brought them out and said, "Sirs, what must I do to be saved?" So they said, "Believe on the Lord Jesus Christ, and you will be saved, you and your household." Then they spoke the word of the Lord to him and to all who were in his house. And he took them the same hour of the night and washed their stripes. And immediately he and all his family were baptized. Now when he had brought them into his house, he set food before them; and he rejoiced, having believed in God with all his household.

**Purpose**:
Resolution, determination, a subject under discussion or action under execution, full intention. Press. **Power**: Ability to act or produce an effect

*Synonym:* Authority, jurisdiction, control, command, to sway it is the ability to will force or substantial influence *Praise:* To express favorable judgment; to glorify God.

*The Bible*:
**Purpose**:
intention, objective. Gods predetermined will.
**Power:**
The strength or authority to act or accomplish something.
**Praise:**
To worship to give honor to.
**Effectual**:
Producing or capable of producing an intended effect; adequate

**"Effectual determined ability to express favorable judgment towards our GOD."**

# PRAISE HAS A FREQUENCY

## Isaiah 60:18 (AB)

*Violence shall no more be heard in your land,*
*nor devastation or destruction within your borders,*
*but you shall call your walls Salvation and your gates Praise.*

Can I share a revelation with you? Praise can be noted to have its own frequency: therefore, noting how often or how loud, now let me say this, I need God on my side at all times, thus I purpose to give praise often and very loud. It can be noted in waves that reach a state of repetitive cycles, so if I stay in the praise zone often, my waves are always oscillating. I can be guaranteed a breakthrough with favors attached. God has given us the OK to render the attack of the enemy powerless. What we need to get, I mean really get, is this; power means to have complete control and all authority over the tactics of the enemy. Praise is the determined ability to produce jurisdiction over the enemy, who is trying to steal your perfected end. Praise is the substantial influence you have when in the presence of the Most High God, to stop the thoughts that come in to kill your destiny.

A great note to be taken here is this, because He dwells in the midst of our praise, we are not alone when we approach our destiny with PRAISE. John 10:10 states he comes only to steal, and to kill, and to destroy. This is his plan. Praise erases his plot.

**"Praise is the executed action that will destroy the one who has come to destroy you."**

**Or**

**"Praise is a prosecuting administrator that will gut the one that has come to gut you."**

# REASONS FOR PRAISE

### Old Testament view:  Exodus 20:5 (NKJV)

*You shall not bow down to them nor serve them. For I, the LORD your God, am a jealous God, visiting the iniquity of the fathers upon the children to the third and fourth generations of those who hate Me,*

### New Testament view: Matthew 4:10 (NKJV)

*Then Jesus said to him, "Away with you, Satan! For it is written, 'You shall worship the LORD your God, and Him only you shall serve.'*

1. He is **GOD**
2. Your salvation is sustained in Praise
3. He paid the Ransom-He paid your debt in full
4. He is mindful of us His thoughts toward us are vast-constant
5. He sits up and dwells where the Praises are
6. He is the rock that's higher than I-He can handle what I can't
7. His mercy endures forever-they are manufactured daily
8. He does not change His mind about us-He is the promise keeper
9. Praise binds up the enemy every time
10. Your victory is in your Praise
11. New mercy and grace with the rising of the sun, even if it's raining
12. The chains that come from the enemy are utterly destroyed proven when HE went to hell in our place and defeated death, hell and the grave. Praise
13. We were created for His Glory & Praise-He liked what He saw and devised a plan
14. It's our reasonable service-Praise
15. He is praying for me daily that my Faith won't fail. He wants me to make it so He set up Praise.

**Praise has a Promise attached to it,
by the Promise Keeper Himself.**

**"Let's activate 0ur praise it works the principle to the Promise."**

# WHAT KEEPS US FROM IT?

## 1. Pride
### Proverbs 11:2 (NKJV)
*When pride comes, then comes shame;But with the humble is wisdom.*

## 2. Guilt/Shame
### Jeremiah 3:25 (NKJV))
*We lie down in our shame, And our reproach covers us.*
*for we have sinned against the LORD our God, we and our fathers,*
*from our youth even to this day, and have not obeyed the voice of the LORD*
*our God."*

## 3. Lack of Faith
### Hebrews 11:6 (NKJV)
*But without faith it is impossible to please Him, for he who comes to God must*
*believe that He is, and that He is a rewarder of those who diligently seek Him.*

## <u>4. Lack of Knowledge and its power</u>
### Hosea 4:6 (KJV)
*My people are destroyed for lack of knowledge: because thou hast rejected*
*knowledge, I will also reject thee, that thou shalt be no priest to me: seeing*
*thou hast forgotten the law of thy God, I will also forget thy children.*

## 5.Your consuming thoughts telling you to keep it down
### James 1:8 (KJV)
*A double minded man is unstable in all his ways.*

## 6.You have been robbed by satanic attack
### John 10:10 (KJV)
*The thief cometh not, but for to steal, and to kill, and to destroy: I am come*
*that they might have life, and that they might have it more abundantly.*

**"This Knowledge obtained can make you free."**
**"Praise is a prayer celebrated out loud."**
**"Turn the volume up on your liberal PRAISE."**

# MADE FOR THIS

### Psalm 66:2 (AB)

*Sing forth the honor and glory of His name; make His praise glorious!*

### Psalm 66:2 (KJV)

*Sing forth the honor of his name: make his praise glorious.*

Your resume in Heaven read on your birthday, and yes, it appears you will be given a position of high honor. That's right; the God of heaven and earth said you meet the criteria to make His praise glorious! Wow! Imagine that He said you were qualified to assist in the earth realm to make Him look as grand as He really is, and to top that, He also stated that He has put you over the works of His hands! We keep the position as long as we live our days praising Him.

**Psalms 150:6~ let everything that has breath praise the Lord.**

The very breath of God created all things (Psalms 33:6), therefore noting that, by our very breath, we should adore Him through our praise. In adoration and humble hearts, we make His praises glorious by the breath He breathed into us to accomplish the job He said we were qualified to do!

**"On judgment day your review will be read, if your praises went up, so shall you."**

CHAPTER SEVEN

# JUST PRAY

## 1 Thessalonians 5:17 (KJV)

*Pray without ceasing.*

WHAT SHOULD I PRAY?

PRAY LIKE HANNAH

CANNOT FAIL

PINNED FOR DANIEL

PRIVATE LANGUAGE

A HEART LIKE DAVID

PRAY ON PURPOSE

# WHAT SHOULD I PRAY?

## Matthew 6:9-13 (NKJV)

*Our Father which art in heaven,*
*Hallowed be Thy name*
*Thy kingdom come*
*Thy will be done*
*On earth as it is in heaven.*
*Give us this day our daily bread*
*And forgive us our debts as we forgive our debtors*
*Lead us not into temptation*
*But deliver us from evil*
*For thine is the kingdom and the power*
*And the glory*
*Forever, and ever.*
***Amen***

**"How one prays determines why one prays. Don't use empty recited words, instead pray with Purpose!"**

# PRAY LIKE HANNAH

## 1 Samuel 2:1-10 (NKJ)

### *Hannah's Prayer*

And Hannah prayed and said,
My heart rejoices in the LORD,
My horn is exalted in the LORD:
I smile at my enemies,
Because I rejoice in Your salvation.  No one is holy like the LORD,
For there is none besides You,
Nor is there any rock like our God. Talk no more so very proudly;
Let no arrogance come from your mouth,
For the LORD is the God of knowledge;
And by Him actions are weighed. "The bows of the mighty men are broken,
And those who stumbled are girded with strength. Those who were full have hired
themselves out for bread,
And the hungry have ceased to hunger.
Even the barren has borne seven,
And she who has many children has become feeble. The LORD kills and makes alive;
He brings down to the grave and brings up. The LORD makes poor and makes rich;
He brings low and lifts up  He raises the poor from the dust
And lifts the beggar from the ash heap,
To set them among princes
And make them inherit the throne of glory
For the pillars of the earth are the LORD's,
And He has set the world upon them.  He will guard the feet of His saints,
But the wicked shall be silent in darkness.
For by strength no man shall prevail. The adversaries of the LORD shall be broken
in pieces;
From heaven He will thunder against them.
The LORD will judge the ends of the earth.
"He will give strength to His king,
and exalt the horn of His anointed."

Have you ever wanted something so badly, that you made a deal with the Maker? This was the case with Hannah; she was barren and in her heart desired to have a child. You see Hannah was the second wife of Elkanah, and while the first wife had children, she taunted Hannah for her lack. Hannah not only asked for something, but in her asking was willing to give her gift back to the Lord for His good and perfect use. Hannah knew that if she prayed and exalted her Lord, that if He so desired, He could open her womb and give her the desire of her heart. The key to her prayer being honored, once she prayed she knew in her heart God had answered, so instead of going back again pleading with the Lord, she blessed His name and rejoiced. God wants us to pray like Hannah, that when we ask Him for something that we are created to do, because He is God, it is already done in heaven, just waiting for us to ask for it, so it can manifest here on earth. God can never go back on His Word, He said be fruitful and multiply, so she asked for something she was created to do, and believed it would come to pass, along with this amazing prayer. God knew the end of Hannah's story, that she would in fact make good on her promise to Him and give her son back to his original maker. God was so faithful that Hannah had 3 other sons and 2 daughters.

**"When we bargain with the maker,
we are sure to get much more than we negotiated for, after all,
He made all that we are asking for."**

# CANNOT FAIL

## Luke 22:31-32 (KJV)

*In addition, the Lord said, Simon, Simon, behold, Satan hath desired to have you, that he may sift you as wheat: but I have prayed for thee, that thy faith fail not: and when thou art converted, strengthen thy brethren.*

Why did Satan desire to try to wear him/us out? The mere fact that Jesus is making intercession for us all, lets us know it is truly because of the greater works you & I will accomplish.

Satan is the bully that everyone is sick of seeing coming in his or her direction. You see, what he desires according to the bible, is to wear us out. The ironic thing is his plot is little by little; let me give you a visual. At the pier of any beach, the waves hit up against it every day. Well over time you don't notice, but the pier has decreased in size, because for years the work of the rough sandy waters has done their job. Well there are three key factors here:

1. Jesus, informed about Satan's plot, tells us that he had to get permission to attempt any sifting.

2. Jesus our Savior will be praying that our faith will not fail.

3. When we have passed through the sifting, encourage someone to give them the strength they will need in their time of sifting. The most POWERful WORDS you can use to remind them is, Jesus has partnered with us so **WE Cannot Fail.**

**"Imagine that the *ONE* who fashioned your destiny, will be praying for you. Since He knows the way you will take, your faith can not fail. *HE* is ever interceding to ensure you do not give up!"**

# PINNED FOR DAVID

## Daniel 10:11-14 (MSG)

*Daniel, he said, man of quality, listen carefully to my message and get up on your feet. Stand at attention. I've been sent to bring you news.' "When he had said this, I stood up, but I was still shaking.*
*Relax, Daniel,' he continued, don't be afraid. From the moment you decided to humble yourself to receive understanding, your prayer was heard, and I set out to come to you., but, was waylaid by the angel-prince of the kingdom of Persia and was delayed for a good three weeks. Michael, one of the chief angel-princes, intervened to help me. I left him there with the prince of the kingdom of Persia. Now I am here to help you understand what will eventually happen to your people. The vision has to do with what's ahead.'*

We have all been in a waiting place where we ponder over and over whether we prayed the right way, or if it is the Lord's will to answer. Maybe we even lost hope in our prayer, not in God, but in our prayer. This story in Daniel just takes my breath away, but at the same time lets me know with certainty, that what is for me, can be delayed, not denied. What's even more profound is the illustration that God allows us to see. He will go to any length to get what's mine to me. The enemy is allowed to do what he is best at, but God will allow him only to go so far before He steps in, or maybe even send back up assistance. However, get this, the place where your blessing was held up, is where He sends the back up, and then your messenger comes with your answered prayer. This story is two fold. One part displays that our prayers are answered when we ask. The gracious Father will make sure we know He heard us, by delivering to us His ultimate plan for our request. Did you get that Michael the **chief** angel was the one sent to assist the messenger? This proves there are some enemies we dare not contend with alone. Your answer may just be waiting to be pinned for its delivery.

**"Don't ever think you're fasting and praying does not have a strong chief back-up plan attached to it."**

# PRIVATE LANGUAGE

### Jude 20 (NIV)

*But you, dear friends, build yourselves up in your most holy faith and pray in the Holy Spirit.*

### Acts 2:6-8 (NIV)

*When they heard this sound, a crowd came together in bewilderment, because each one heard them speaking in his own language. Utterly amazed, they asked: "Are not all these men who are speaking Galileans? Then how is it that each of us hears them in his own native language?*

### Romans 8:26-27 (NIV)

*In the same way, the Spirit helps us in our weakness. We do not know what we ought to pray for, but the Spirit himself intercedes for us with groans that words cannot express. And he who searches our hearts knows the mind of the Spirit, because the Spirit intercedes for the saints in accordance with God's will.*

We will forever get in the way, so step aside and let the Spirit of the Lord reveal to us His plans, and make way for what HE really has in store for us. Think about it, when you pray, because you only know what you desire for your flesh, this is how we pray, but if in fact, you were made privy to a private language that in no ways could be intercepted, would you not take that prayerful route? The flesh is only hungry for what it is familiar with, so this is how we approach our secret place, and in turn, is upset when our prayers avail nothing. I know that my Father desires for me to have the best, so I purpose to get all that He has for me. In order for this to be made possible, I must allow His spirit which resides in me, to tap into the throne room, and get a peak of the plan and deliver it to me from heaven to earth which is where I reside. One other fascinating revelation of my private language is that it is private, no one but my Father alone, can interpret and MAKE it come to pass. His ways, are not our ways. His ways, brings us to the perfected end that He planned for our absolute abundant end.

The enemy no matter how he tries cannot take notes when I pray in my private language. Therefore, my prayer in my private language, may not be held up, or altered in anyway. No delays, No denies, for I am doing it according to the plan. When we follow these instructions and begin to see the manifestations, others will be amazed, and it will be here we can once again testify.

**"My private Language guarantees no interception."**

# A HEART LIKE DAVID

## Acts 13:22 (MSG)

*"Up to the time of Samuel the prophet, God provided judges to lead them. Then they asked for a king, and God gave them Saul, son of Kish, out of the tribe of Benjamin. After Saul had ruled forty years, God removed him from office and put King David in his place, with this commendation: 'I've searched the land and found this David, son of Jesse. He's a man whose heart beats to my heart, a man who will do what I tell him.'*

Betrayer, liar, adulterer, murderer, giant killer, poet, and shepherd. These are the characteristics of the man God said, his "heart beats to my heart." King David, son of Jesse, in the lineage of Christ, had like all of us a serious flesh issue. But in spite of all this, he was hand selected by the creator of heaven and earth. It is for these reasons that our Father in heaven gave His only Son.

Yet the question remains, why did God say that David was a man after His own heart, or like the translation used here, "his heart beats to my heart?" Psalms 51:10 says it best. David asked God to create in him a clean heart, and renew a steadfast spirit within him. What a powerful request. David knew that in order for his heart to be made new, and his spirit revived, he must take it to the One who created it. He was aware that only God could do it for him. After all, He is truly the Creator; no one, not you nor I, have the ability to go in and remanufacture one's own heart. David was sorry for what he had done, but most importantly, for whom he had sinned against.

David's motivation was to stay in right standing with his heavenly Father. His objective was clear. God had proven Himself faithful on David's behalf time after time, and he knew David's heart was pure towards Him. David knew that he only became who he was by God's grace.

In the translation, God said, David "was a man that would do whatever I tell him." God took the shepherd boy from the field, anointed him with oil, and gifted and equipped him for the battle which in the end made him King.

Where you are today, can God say, "(**your name here**) is a woman/man after my heart?"

**"A clean heart is critical; a steadfast spirit will keep your heart clean."**

# PRAY ON PURPOSE

## Acts 16:25-29 (NIV)

*About midnight Paul and Silas were praying and singing hymns to God, and the other prisoners were listening to them. Suddenly there was such a violent earthquake that the foundations of the prison were shaken. At once all the prison doors flew open, and everybody's chains came loose.*

I wonder often what would manifest in our midst if we just for once, really approached the throne with true expectation. Imagine for just a moment if you approached the One whom said you could have what you ask in HIS name if we just believed in what He said was in fact true. Let's look from this perspective; how long have you been in your own prison?, has it been over 5 minutes you have been in a ditch someone dug for you Joseph?, have you had more than your share of vain imagination, that at the end of the day worked harder than you did?. Let's try this one on for size, the ones you came to ensure life eternal, devise a plot to take yours by way of a rugged cross. If we are true to ourselves, I believe we all would agree that all the situations noted above require a purposeful prayer. The strategies were clear they all were meant to cause a catatonic reaction, however because we know these are the cases that the father wants us to ask Him to assist, we invite His will to be done. Gods order never changes, sure He could fix all the plots that come against us but, we must invite HIM in. When we do there can manifest an earthquake, prison doors can be suddenly unlocked without the use of keys, chains loosed, you may even go from a ditch to a palace, your imaginations can be reset to things on high, your very cross may get you a seat in glory next to your Father.

Whatever your expectation, you cannot witness the manifestation until you pray on purpose with purpose.

**Pray: appeal, devotion, grace, and plea.**
**Purpose: intention, desire, aim, and destination**
**There's an intention to our appeal.**
**A great desire for devotion.**
**Aiming for our grace.**

**Making a strong plea towards our destination.~**
**PRAY WITH PURPOSE ON PURPOSE**

CHAPTER EIGHT

# LOVE

## Song of Solomon 2:4 (AB)

*He brought me to the banqueting house, and his banner over me was love [for love waved as a protecting and comforting banner over my head when I was near him].*

LOVE IN ACTION

558 TIMES

SO LOVED

THIS LOYAL LOVE

GREATEST QUALITY

HELPLESS IN LOVE

LISTENING IN LOVE

BOTTLED'EM UP

FIRST LOVE

TABLE FOR TWO

# LOVE IN ACTION

## Romans 5:8 (NKJV)

*"But God demonstrates His own love toward us, in that while we were still sinners, Christ died for us."*

**1. Love explains why God creates-because He loves, He creates people to love.**
**2. Why God cares-because He loves them.**
**3. He even loves sinful people- we have a free will.**
**4. Because of Christ love for us He died for us-His love for us compelled Him to seek a solution to the problem of sin.**
**5. Love is the reason we receive eternal life. God love expresses itself to us forever.**

As a people, we have contaminated the Word, by believing that it is a feeling, but in reality, to love is a choice and an action. The Holy Spirit is the action part of God, therefore; here is where our source of power to love is found. God's love always involves choice and action. The Holy Spirit brings life to that spirit who responds to his voice with great determination, and effort. Because He is love, He is our true source, He is our life, He made the effort, and we must make the choice.

**Choice: determination; option; voice; preference ~ Action: life; response; spirit; effort**

**"God's love for us caused Him to make a choice that brought us life; the action was the preference of the Cross."**

**Jesus' love for us drove Him to take action at the CROSS~**

# 558 TIMES

## 1 John 4:16 (NIV)

*And so we know and rely on the love God has for us.*
*God is love. Whoever lives in love, lives in God, and God in him.*
**GOD is love.**

**Love** or anything associated with it, is mentioned in the Bible 558 times. Jesus Christ demonstrated how to show true love. He exemplified God's love for humanity. He showed true love through His focus on self-sacrifice, the seeking of the well-being and benefit of others at one's own expense. That is true love!

He loved us not because we were lovable or worthy of that love, but because He is the personification of true love. God Himself has demonstrated the greatness of Godly love, true love. The Master teacher has taught us.

## 1 Thessalonians 4:9 (AB)

*But concerning brotherly love [for all other Christians], you have no need to*
*have anyone write you, for you yourselves have been [personally] taught by*
*God to love one another.*
*5 ~ Serve  &  8 ~ Put off*
*558*

**'So serve one another in Love and put off the old man."**

# SO LOVED

## John 3:16 (MSG)

*"This is how much God loved the world: He gave his Son, his one and only Son. And this is why: so that no one need be destroyed; by believing in him, anyone can have a whole and lasting life. God did not go to all the trouble of sending his Son merely to point an accusing finger, telling the world how bad it was. He came to help, to put the world right again. Anyone who trusts in him is acquitted; anyone who refuses to trust him has long since been under the death sentence without knowing it. In addition, why? Because of that person's failure to believe in the one-of-a-kind Son of God when introduced to him.*

There is not much to be stated. However, questions arise in my mind, so let me paint a picture before I strike my big blow. One year my son played the crucified Christ. When I saw Jaylon coming down the isle with a cross on his back, imitation blood dripping from his tiny little face, food coloring on his torn Hanes t-shirt, his made to believe sad eyes, the crowd shouting crucify him, crucify him, I was done and convinced, because I know me better than anyone except God, I would not have sent Jaylon to die, at least not for me. I mean think about it, your thorn, would you be willing to send your child or one of your loved ones for you, knowing that the thorn you have they died for, so that you could live, yet you kept on taking the grace because it has been freely given?  In fact, you tailored your issue to suit your need, and you pondered on the grace you knew God would so willingly give, but not for long. Your thorn at the moment was greater than your love for your loved one. Mad is what you would be at the thought of someone taking for granted your sacrifice for them. Well, it's what we do everyday, would your response be different if you were the one who sent the ONE to die?

**"The One who so Loved, Gave HIS best."**

**Pray that you can give your best.**

# THIS LOYAL LOVE

## Lamentations 3:23 (MSG)

*God's loyal love couldn't have run out,*
*his merciful love couldn't have dried up.*
*They're created new every morning.*

Only HE knows the road that I will take, to get me to my original designated end. For He is the MASTER navigator. HIS ways will forever be higher than ours. I bless HIM for the journey. This road I am on, will get me to my eternal end…His throne room in Glory… and that puts me at HIS feet forever. The only possible way for it to come to pass, is HIS awesome extension of GRACE & MERCY that is distributed and manufactured in the Heavenly place daily, with us in mind.

**"This Navigation gets me to my Destination even in TRAFFIC, and I get there on TIME."**

# GREATEST QUALITY

### 1 Corinthians 13:1-3 (NKJV)
### The Greatest Gift

*Though I speak with the tongues of men and of angels, but have not love, I have become sounding brass or a clanging cymbal. And though I have the gift of prophecy, and understand all mysteries and all knowledge, and though I have all faith, so that I could remove mountains, but have not love, I am nothing. And though I bestow all my goods to feed the poor, and though I give my body to be burned, but have not love, it profits me nothing.*

**Love** is mentioned more times in the bible than the actual cross, you know the place our savior died, but it was love that drove Him to it. God told us in 1 Corinthians 13. The entire chapter is dedicated to LOVE. In this particular book, Paul stresses that without LOVE, all else is failed. The love he speaks of is unselfish in all aspects. God gives us spiritual gifts for our natural life, when we get to heaven, there will be no need for these gifts. We as a people have truly gotten the word mixed up, so much so, that we have almost corrupted the main point. We say it in passing, we say it because someone else says it, we say it out of obligation, we say it to get what we want, being selfish. Paul states here, that the greatest human quality one can have is LOVE. I think most of us would agree that if Paul stresses that love is a quality, and John say's that God is Love, then clearly speaking it is this, to achieve such a characteristic, gives us all we will ever need, from beginning to end. God has given us the unique ability to reflect His true character.

**"Grade A is what WE have, when WE chose to _Love._"**

# HELPLESS IN LOVE

### Romans 5:6 (NKJV)

*For when we were still without strength, in due time Christ died for the ungodly.*

Imagine that the maker of Heaven and Earth decided to die for us while we were weak, feeble, helpless, nerveless, powerless, helpless, and terminally ill. The ultimate factor is this, we were in sin, because just in case you didn't know, the above synonyms listed, really are the result of a life without salvation. The coined phrase that stands out to me and I pray to you is, terminally ill. In other words, destined for the grave. God in His infinite mercy and grace, yet again devised a strategy that would conquer death, hell, all sickness, diseases and the grave. He in fact, took our place while He himself was yet without sin, even took our place in hell for 3 days! I would still rather spend one day in His court, than a thousand elsewhere.

### What a Savior?

### "Thank Him for targeting your illness, that in His death we were made Strong."

# LISTENING IN LOVE

## James 1:22-25 (MSG)

*Don't fool yourself into thinking that you are a listener when you are anything but, letting the Word go in one ear and out the other. Act on what you hear! Those who hear and don't act are like those who glance in the mirror, walk away, and two minutes later have no idea who they are, what they look like.*

*But whoever catches a glimpse of the revealed counsel of God—the free life!—even out of the corner of his eye, and sticks with it, is no distracted scatterbrain but a man or woman of action. That person will find delight and affirmation in the action.*

Ron my husband has been for years telling Chelsea and Jaylon, the Lord gave us 2 ears and 1 mouth so that we could listen more than we speak. Take heed. Sometimes the most profound thing has never been spoken. Yet the revelations we get from listening, will astound you and those watching. We are all teachers in this life, and those that do not look in the mirror and forget what they just learned, learn the greatest lessons, and they take careful notes to ensure they really past the test. The notes are found in the Word.

**"The test is in the listening, not just the note taking, it's the listening that proves you are still teachable."**

# FIRST LOVE

## 1 John 4:10 (KJV)

*Herein is love, not that we loved God, but that he loved us, and sent his Son*
*to be the propitiation for our sins.*

We all at some point in our life, we had that first crush, that we swore was love, like most of us, we doodled that crushes name right next to ours. It is all we could think about; therefore it's all we talked about. Cute to ponder over, but the fact of the matter is this; the One who crushed on us first, is still crushing on us. God has an amazing kind of love. In fact, I could just see the day He doodled my name next to His, on heavenly paper, posted all over the throne, God loves Theresa.

It is only because He loved me first that I am even able to love Him or anyone for that matter. The Holy Spirit is what leads, governs and guides me to tap into those parts that only He can teach how to function in and through me. Posted notes in Glory with your name on them, doodled by the Master Lover.

**"Grateful for the Doodling." God loves (_your name here_).**

# TABLE FOR TWO

## Psalm 136:25 (KJV)

*Who giveth food to all flesh: for his mercy endureth for ever.*

A wonderful table set before you, with the finest china, that heaven has to offer. Magnificent stemware, He went all out just for you. Not the normal silverware, but the 18kt flatware. There is a beautiful candelabrum with three burning stems on a white linen tablecloth, and the centerpiece arrangement is the Rose of Sharon and the Lily of the Valley. The feast He prepared with you in mind, on the menu is first course life, second course security, third course peace, and for dessert there is abundant grace drenched with a marvelous healing patina. What a banquet, the Master Chef has so carefully composed for your intimate time together. Every detail strategically put in place; He even sent you a private invitation;

Greetings from the throne room, our Lord God almighty has cordially requested your presence at a Banquet in Glory.

Please <u>RSVP</u>.

Master Chef request that regrets need not reply.

Yes/Amen ⁓ ✅

Maybe/Perchance ⁓

No/Deny ⁓

**"The Candelabras burning are eternal; they represent the Father, Son, & the Holy Ghost."**

## CHAPTER NINE

# MERCY

## Romans 9:15 (CEV)

*The Lord told Moses that he has pity and mercy on anyone he wants to.*

CHARACTER ASSASSINATION

THE CALL BETRAYED

SQUEEZE ME BUT PLEASE DO NOT FREEZE ME

NO MORE BLOOD

SPECIAL DELIVERY

MEDIATE ON HIS WORKS

NOTICE OF EVICTION

# CHARACTER ASSASSINATION

### Jeremiah 18:19 (NIV)

*Listen to me, O LORD; hear what my accusers are saying!*

**An attack intended to ruin someone's reputation [syn: character assassination]**
**To kill suddenly or secretively, esp. a politically prominent person; murder premeditatedly and treacherously.**
**To destroy or harm treacherously and viciously:**
***to assassinate a person's character.***

We serve a great big God, think about it, HE knows all that there is to know about us, even the things we have yet to admit to ourselves, and yet HE still loves us. Think about it, the one who knows all, sees all, did I say **ALL**, and well it is true. But yet, HE does not tear us down. So why then, do we do it to our brothers & sisters and even ourselves? The truth of the matter is, that none of us even know the whole story, but the One who does, extends to us daily mercy, and that amazing grace.

**"We should learn from the One who knows the whole story."**

# THE CALL BETRAYED

## Judges 16:18-20 (NIV)

*When Delilah saw that he had told her everything, she sent word to the rulers of the Philistines, "Come back once more; he has told me everything." So the rulers of the Philistines returned with the silver in their hands. Having put him to sleep on her lap, she called a man to shave off the seven braids of his hair, and so began to subdue him. And his strength left him. Then she called, "Samson, the Philistines are upon you!"*
*He awoke from his sleep and thought, "I'll go out as before and shake myself free." But he did not know that the LORD had left him*

Samson, so caught up into his own plan, that he forgot God's plan. He had permitted a Philistine woman to rob him of his preordained partnership with the Lord. There are three pivotal factors here: #1 Samson allowed the same plot to trick him once more; his wife had pleaded with him once before ( Judges 14:17). In spite of the danger, this posed to shut her pestering off, so he gave in, which means he did not learn the first time. #2 Samson broke covenant with God, and his wife. Samson only had this remarkable strength, because of his consecrated life to God, but in the heat the moment, he left God out. To his wife, he broke the marriage covenant when he went in to the Harlot (Delilah), and she used all of her female woes to make him WEAK. #3 Samson did not know that the Lord had left him; he was so accustomed to the Lord being ever present with him, that he did not realize he was trying to combat this enemy on his own, like only reading the Word on Sunday, presuming that it will keep you all week. Samson's strength gone was one thing, but he wasn't aware that God's presence was gone as well! God could have restored it if he chose to. This was proven in the end when Samson asked God to let him take vengeance for his eyes that the Philistines had gauged out. God honored his plea. Samson killed more at the time of his death than he did all of his life!

**"Never let your own desires lead you to Betrayal."**

# SQUEEZE *ME* BUT PLEASE DO *NOT* FREEZE *ME*

## Genesis 50:20 (KJV)

*But as for you, ye thought evil against me; but God meant it unto good, to bring to pass, as it is this day, to save much people alive*
.

**Squeeze:**
To press hard;  Extract by applying pressure; To cram
**Freeze:**
To fix at current level; To stay.

We have all been in a position, where we have told our testimony, the real one. There are benefits to this, and then there are some downs to it. The problem is, that the story that we shared, they try to keep us there, never giving us the benefit that, that was then, this is now. This is what I call freezing. The most important piece here is that the testimony was obtained, only because of the squeezing that we endured. If we were smart, we would understand that everything has opportunity for change and growth, and that we should make room for them both.

**Every man has *HIS-TORY*…..**

**I can take the squeezing, but no more freezing. I am *Free!***

# NO MORE BLOOD
## ATONEMENT

### Leviticus 17:11 (NKJV)

*For the life of the flesh is in the blood, and I have given it to you upon
the altar to make atonement for your souls; for it is the blood that makes
atonement for the soul.'*

Atonement comes from the Hebrew "Kippurim," which means to cover over. Covering over sin, by making an equivalent ransom or sacrifice, so that adequate recompense is made for the offense. Jesus Christ our Lord and Savior did the same for us when He chose the nails and the cross for our sins, so that we are able to go to the Father at any given time, because of His shed blood. This sacrifice provided a promise, as well as a full payment for our daily sin nature, coupled with mercy, that would ensure that all who chose to believe in Him, would have everlasting life. All because God desired to save us, and forgive us our sins, and ultimately reconcile us back to Him. God provided atonement for us when He manifested Himself in the flesh, and died a human death. The blood that was shed on Calvary, is the blood we need to live, for it was this blood that hit the mercy seat which grants the new mercies you see daily. Without atonement, we would suffer the wrath of the sins we so willfully subject ourselves to daily.

**Imagine if you were told that there is *no more blood* (mercy).**

**"Our life needs all the Blood Jehovah-Jireh (provider) put on
the mercy seat in Glory."**

# SPECIAL DELIVERY

## Isaiah 55:11(MSG)

*So will the words that come out of my mouth not come back empty-handed.*
*They'll do the work I sent them to do; they'll complete the assignment I gave them.*

No need to muse over empty words spoken, the fact of the matter is this, there is no such thing. Word's have a life all their own, why else would the Word clearly say life and death is in the power of the tongue? So is the same for the birthright (purpose) we each have. While studying the above text, the Lord allowed me to get a glimpse of His date book. Like most books, it had a copyright year, and if I remember correctly, it was something like 1BC, printed and published in Heavens Throne; all the rights were reserved for the Master. The only thing that was different was that this book only had 3 contributors; they were the Father, Son, and the Holy Ghost. To top that, it comes with a lifetime guarantee; oh did I mention that His date book actually had a title, Destiny.

Wondering what my point is, well I am glad you asked. Because the date book is dated long before your natural birthday, every plan that He has made for your life must be accomplished, and He has a set delivery date, nothing can stop it. Trust and know that the Angels whom have been sent to watch over you, have a C.O.D ledger that will ensure your destiny is not missed. The purpose of the C.O.D. is this; they cannot come back to the throne and say you were not home. They must hover until you sign the will, because here is the greater scheme of the matter, His will for you was dated before the foundations of the world, before you were formed. Because all that He does has a purpose, please note to self, your life has a purpose that MUST accomplish that which HE said. The signature line on the C.O.D. ledger cannot be void.

**"Special Delivery, signature needed to accept the Will from the Master."**
**Please sign here_____**
**Date has already been registered in Glory on your Birthday.**

# WE HAVE GOOD STALKERS

## Psalms 23:6 (MSG)

*Your beauty and love chase after me every day of my life.*
*I'm back home in the house of GOD for the rest of my life.*

## ~ (KJV) ~

*Surely, goodness and mercy shall follow me all the days of my life: and I will*
*dwell in the house of the LORD forever.*

## Stalker:
Pursue obsessively, to the point of harassment **to make sure
the presence is known.**

What an exciting thing to know, that the ONE whom is stalking
us does it with an absolute purpose in mind, to ensure that we
dwell with HIM in glory forever. Mercy and goodness here denote
the Father's loyal love to us as HIS children. Follow describes an
intense pursuit to get us to be forever in HIS presence. Another
way to applaud this scripture with a voice of triumph is this; we
have a stalker who offers us protection, as in the Secret Service.
HE is always there with the perfect weapons to ensure our safety
and they are Goodness & Mercy.

**"I do not mind being stalked, by the ONE who directs my
path for HE will help me."**

# MEDITATE ON HIS WORKS

## Psalm 77:12 (NKJV)

*I will also meditate on all Your work, and talk of Your deeds.*

**Meditate**: deep respect and awe, to brood over, dream about and entertain in our thoughts.

The fact of the matter is this, by our acknowledgment of Him, shows we Love Him. Think of it this way, when we really want something, we always figure out away to get it. I want our Father to always remember my works big or small, and when I meditate on His works, I credit Him as Lord and Creator; He then credits me as a worthy friend and a citizen of heaven!

**"His works are beautiful and worthy of meditating on often."**

# NOTICE OF EVICTION
## (you have been served to <u>Bounce</u>)

### Revelation 12:9 (ESV)

*And the great dragon was thrown down, that ancient serpent, who is called the devil and Satan, the deceiver of the whole world-he was thrown down to the earth, and his angels were thrown down with him.*

When we have seen the Lord of host, when we have tasted and seen just how well He has been we are to praise Him. We are not to rally against Him. You see the worship leader in Glory thought himself more highly than he ought; what a ridiculous thought. This would be the equivalent to someone trying to get credit for your good works. The Word tells us that we are to give honor where honor is due, God never changes His plan or mind where we are concerned, so why then do we attempt to do it. If the original plan was praise leader, then worship with all that you have, if you are to intercede pray with all your power which has been given, if your role is teacher teach His word not your own, nursery worker in your local body nurture the children according to His plan, and curriculum not one you devised. Satan fights us all day, everyday for the mistake he made, and is frustrated that what he was called to do, he no longer has the ability to occupy that seat, or office. God called the warring parties together in heaven and in His Terrible voice said get him out of glory, so Michael and his army, did just that. Asta la vista partner, chow, adios, avoir, peace out, however you purpose to phrase this farewell I am positive of this I would never want to experience the Master getting a war started that in the end would  result in my eviction notice.

**"Praise is our role, heaven will be our gain. Make good on these payments so you will not be evicted by the land-LORD."**

## CHAPTER TEN

# SOME THINGS
# MADE PLAIN

## John 3:16 (NIV)

*"For God so loved the world that he gave his one and only Son, that whoever believes in him shall not perish but have eternal life.*

SOMETHING'S IN MY EYE

HIS ICU

PATCH THE HOLE

LEAVE IT BEHIND

THE MEANTIMES

FRIENDSHIP LOYALTY

MY BROTHER MY SAVIOR

WHO IS MAN THAT?

CAKE MIX THEORY

OBSOLETE

PRAYER OF SALVATION

TIME TO UNDRESS

# SOMETHING'S IN MY EYE

## Matthew 7:3-5 (NKJV)

*For with what judgment you judge, you will be judged; and with the measure you use, it will be measured back to you. And why do you look at the speck in your brother's eye, but do not consider the plank in your own eye? Or how can you say to your brother, 'Let me remove the speck from your eye'; and look, a plank is in your own eye? 5 Hypocrite! First remove the plank from your own eye, and then you will see clearly to remove the speck from your brother's eye.*

Every judgment that people make becomes a basis for their own judgment. The scripture text is kindly saying to us deal with our own matters, and stop seeking to criticize the next person for their faults. Verse six makes it clear just how urgent this plea is to us by calling us hypocrites for taking such posture; while I studied this portion of scripture I thought of how as a child our parents would tell us what our punishment would look like if we did this or that. When Jesus says in verse two the same measure you judge so shall you be judged, *OUCH.* What more needs to be said, one of the things I have come to love about God so much is how He has carefully set up our instructions to ensure we get back to Him. In the book of Luke 22:32, Jesus tells Peter that Satan desires to sift him as wheat, but He in the same breath tells him that when you have come through strengthen your brother. The illustration is the same here in this portion of scripture for in verse 5 Jesus says get the plank out of your own eye before you cast a critical opinion on your brother or sister in the body or just in this world, because He created us all we are all His children. A punishment from our parents is one thing but if you are like me, I do not want to suffer any type of retribution from my Father in heaven. I believe that this is a perfect example of the fear of the Lord is the start of wisdom Proverbs 9:10. My mother often told us as children to be careful about what we say about others at 43 I understand. Thanks Mom for the lesson, and for every callous word I uttered from my mouth out of ignorance. Father I repent.

**"The measuring stick of GOD I am certain is long, and I am fearful for its WRATH."**

# HIS ICU

### Malachi 4:2 (AB)

*But unto you who revere and worshipfully fear My name shall the Sun of Righteousness arise with healing in His wings and His beams, and you shall go forth and gambol like calves [released] from the stall and leap for joy.*

Imagine yourself naked on the surgeons table in the operating room. There are more than just the doctor and yourself present, there is a team of medical personnel most of which you may have never seen before, but because you understand that in order for you to be made 100%, you undress in preparation for your needed healing. The first step to a successful surgery is not the first cut, but in your conviction that causes you to confess you are imperfect, ill at heart, feeble, suffering, weak, tired, broken, delicate, troubled, struggling, tormented, not whole, have real issues, or just sick.

God offers a procedure daily to us for all the above ailments, by manufacturing new mercies to each new day we see. However, He cannot heal what we hide in the secret places of our hearts and minds. Before we go any further, let me tell you the most exciting, yet vital key to this outpatient process; you will not be alone. You will from this day forward, be in HIS intensive care unit, where HE will monitor your every progressions and occasional digressions. What an amazing surgeon we have, Heavens case manager checked, and the fee for this operation was paid in full, so why walk away with a band-aid, or torn gauze oozing with yesterday's cuts and bruises, when we can stay in HIS icu( I see you) to be certain that all the care we need is found in HIS *wing?*.

**Psalm 91:4 (GNT) He will cover you with His wings; you will be safe in His care; His faithfulness will protect and defend you.**

**The great physician is critical about our urgent care.**

**ICU~"I see you and I will never leave you or forsake you."**

# PATCH THE HOLE

## Song of Solomon 2:15 (NCV)

*Catch the foxes for us—*
*the little foxes that ruin the vineyards*
*while they are in blossom.*

We are all so quick to think that if there is a problem, it has been predicated on some major past or present circumstance which we allowed ourselves to fall so quickly into. Or perhaps the Lord is getting us back, for some besetting thing. Well the truth of the matter is this, maybe, just maybe it's the thing we were not willing to consider an issue, or that it should concern us in our salvation: Case and point, though it may be a small matter to you, just think for a moment what it must matter to GOD, if HE clearly told us that it's the little foxes that spoil the vine, if this was not so, HE would not have put it in HIS word (*will* ) for us to read. When a will is being read, all viable parties are asked to be present.

**"Make sure you are present at the reading, to ensure you receive your portion. *The Promise.*"**

# LEAVE IT BEHIND

### Genesis 19:26 (KJV)

*But his wife looked back behind him, and she became a pillar of salt*

She left her stuff at the prison where her enemy took resident….but she said, I forgive you. The tire went flat, and she had time to think, and made the decision to leave her past. When we realize where we were trapped by our past, or the place we got stuck, it is interesting to find, that if we pay close attention, we will recognize the power we have to leave it. Often, we continue to carry, only what was needed for a moment, a moment that was only intended for our spiritual growth, nothing more and nothing less. So drop the baggage...... like most of us, we drop it, we leave it, only to pick it up again. A friend once told me that, when we give our issues to GOD, but then we go back and pick it up, we are trespassing, therefore we are in violation. Why? Because we have now stepped into territory that was, and forever will be, off limits. Because if we were able to fix it, we wouldn't had to leave it in the first place. My son once asked me," why is there a devil?" My answer though simple to me, has become more profound today. JESUS is the reason. For without HIM, there would be no need for an enemy to war against us... leave it... for this reason HE came.

**Our trial ceases when we are no longer reluctant to leave it with the One who fashioned it for our good.**

# THE MEANTIMES

## Psalm 37:7 (NIV)

*Be still before the LORD and wait patiently for him; do not fret when men
succeed in their ways, when they carry out their wicked schemes.*

Welcome to the microwave generation. What I would like to
emphasize here, is WAITING. To wait involves an expectation, and
is based on knowledge and trust. Waiting is for some, taking action
at the right time, and for others, it simply means resting in the Lord.
I am with the ladder part of this summation, because it is here that
we must know the One whom we are waiting on, so we must be
content in His timing and His provision; in other words, be content
that the answer will come. But would you agree, that it is in the
meantimes where we twiddle our fingers, dot every i, cross every t,
smile at every stranger we see on the streets, as if this will cause the
waiting process to not have to be sooooooooo long?

**There are 7 benefits to our waiting; I would like to shed some of
these revelations:**

### 7 – Gods perfect number.

1. Honor God by our faith
2. Makes us aware of strength we have
3. Builds character
4. Learn who we are
5. Gives us a reason to Praise
6. Encourages others, to increase their desire to know the ONE we
   are waiting on
7. Makes the enemy twiddle his fingers, cross every t and dot every i

If you are like most believers, you recognize that the God we serve, is so much bigger than our mind's imagination could really fathom. The Father actually created a plan for our meantimes, that in all circumstances everything works out for our good, and without any doubt, for His ultimate glory. **Jeremiah 29:11 he declares, "For I know the thoughts that I think toward you, says the LORD, thoughts of peace and not of evil, to give you a future and a hope."** Here is the key to keeping your mind clear of everyday interferences, understand that the plans he is speaking about were not jotted down the day you were introduced to your now sudden chaos, but in fact they were written before you were conceived The idea that the Lord of all considered you special enough to create a victorious end to our meantimes is yet again another reason for us to praise Him with the fruit of our lips. The meantimes are needed for our lesson in waiting. The waiting teaches us not to lean on our own understanding, but to look to the one who has our perfected end carefully mapped out.

**"Wait in your meantimes, looking up not leaning down."**

# FRIENDSHIP LOYALTY
## SAUL ~ DAVID ~ JONATHAN ~JESUS

### 1 Samuel 18:3 (NIV)

*Jonathan made a covenant with David because he loved him as himself.*

The power of connections is pivotal, to where we must go, as well as where we have already been. If you think about it, there was someone in your past that lined you up for this very moment. Jonathan and David, such an amazing story about loyalty, self-worth, and friendship, as well as love, honor and at the end of it all, respect. Understand that Jonathan was Saul's son, and because of Saul's heart for David, Jonathan the prince would not inherit the kingdom. Can you imagine walking with the one, who if time allowed, would take your place? Jonathan knew this, yet he remained faithful to his friend. Some may ask how, the answer to this relationship far exceeds our imagination. Jonathan and David remained faithful to God and their relationship to one another, for this reason only, were they able to handle what was to come. At the end of the day, neither Jonathan nor David allowed their flesh to rise up and wreak havoc. Our Father in heaven has allowed us to connect with someone, somewhere, for such a time as this, and if we are wise, we will stand up quickly and say thanks. You see Jonathan and David were confident in the Father. How do I say this with such conviction? Simply put, they knew if they took care of God's business as He planned, He must take care of them. The bottom line was their obedience to God, and loyalty to each other. Jonathan was so committed to David, that ultimately he would spare him from his father Saul… we need to know that God honors loyalty (faith), obedience, faithfulness, and love.

**Recognize your Divine Connection, I guarantee it will lead you to God's family ~**

**Look at David & Jesus ~**

# MY BROTHER MY SAVIOR

### Hebrews 4:15 (NKJV)

*For we do not have a High Priest who cannot sympathize with our weaknesses, but was in all points tempted as we are, yet without sin.*

### Hebrews 4:15 (MSG)

*Now that we know what we have—Jesus, this great High Priest with ready access to God—let us not let it slip through our fingers. We do not have a priest who is out of touch with our reality. He has been through weakness and testing, experienced it all—all but the sin. So let us walk right up to him and get what he is so ready to give. Take the mercy,*
*Accept the help.*

Our Lord and Savior was the ideal human; fully prepared. The ideal human was now ready to live a perfect life. Look closely at this human we call Savior, he was born to a mother naturally, He had emotional outburst, He got angry, He cried real tears, and for the record, our Savior even had moments of fear, even though He ultimately knew the outcome. He was born to die. He died and was resurrected on the third day. He cared for the ones no one else was even concerned about, i.e.: women such as Elizabeth, the widow of Nain, the sinner who anointed His feet, the woman searching for the lost coin. He even mentions the social outcast, such as the Gentiles, Shepherds, the poor, the lepers and let us not forget the sinners; you and me, whom He died for while we were yet sinners. The humanity of Jesus can be visually seen as well as experienced as we take time to read His Word, it is here that we will come into the knowledge of His humanness, where we will have the opportunity to witness His weariness, dependence, grief, His anguish, and then take a moment to witness His death.

**"Our Brother, the innocent, put to death after His human experience. The result; His humanness took Him to a cross that made Him Savior."**

# WHO IS MAN THAT?

## Hebrews 2:6-8 (NKJV)

*But one testified in a certain place, saying: What is man that You are mindful of him Or the son of man that You take care of him? You have made him a little lower than the angels; You have crowned him with glory and honor And set him over the works of Your hands*

Think for a moment about the job description of an angel, a glorious position to sit and worship all day at the throne, and maybe sometimes be put on assignment to deliver a blessing to one of the Father's faithful children. Nevertheless, it is us here, in the human form, which God has actually chosen to rule over all His creation. The Father has selected us in our sinful nature to show the angels, as if they do not know, that He keeps His promises. Because we know in Genesis, He proclaimed that He has put us over the works of His hands. It is only because of our current sinful state that, as noted in the scripture "but now we do not yet see all things under him" the only way we have any authority, is when we activate the power of the Holy Ghost. Otherwise, we in our sinful nature, have no power to come against subjects in the earth, because we are the same. Therefore, I totally understand the question of the angels asking, "Who is man that you are so mindful of him?" For goodness sakes, the angels do what they are told, never having to ask for forgiveness, or seeking faith. God is faithful, so of course He will visit with us; He must, to ensure that the Word will perform what it is suppose to accomplish. I am curious about one thing, which angel had the courage to go and ask God that question? I can clearly see them saying, "you go, no you go."

**"The plan from Genesis to Hebrews has not changed; we *shall* rule over the works of the Masters hand, it is part of His great plan."**

# CAKE MIX THEORY

## Galatians 5:22-26 (NKJV)

*But the fruit of the Spirit is love, joy, peace, longsuffering, kindness, good-ness, faithfulness, gentleness, self-control. Against such there is no law. And those who are Christ's have crucified the flesh with its passions and desires. If we live in the Spirit, let us also walk in the Spirit. Let us not become con-ceited, provoking one another, envying one another.*

Let's go baking, the ingredients we need to make the perfect cake is; eggs, milk, butter, bowl, flour, sugar, vanilla, measuring cup, and of course a mixer. My grandmother told me to make sure to follow the directions on every recipe; otherwise, it will not provide you with the tasty treat you intended, when you started on the baking journey. I had a good friend, who would always bring me yummy treats, banana bread, and pumpkin-bars. If I saw the foil while she was coming through the door, I knew I was in for a treat especially baked by her mother, just for me. Well one day to my surprise, Laura Wagoner my treat bearer, instead of the baked goods, she handed over the recipe to me, to do all the baking I wanted.

Here's where grandma's rule mattered most, after 5 or 6 tries, ready to give up, my husband said, "what is the problem?" My bread was like a chewy cookie dough contraption. I told him I was doing everything right, he replied, "You can not be." So Ron had me read out loud to him, all the ingredients, and when I did, to my surprise, there was the culprit of my failed banana bread; I was using baking powder instead of baking soda. I am now the banana bread queen. The lesson, while it was in the natural, so it is for us in spirit. You see without the baking soda, the bread could not rise, if I have 8 of the ingredients to the fruit of the Spirit, one less than is required, I cannot rise. What is more powerful is we have had the recipe in our possession for over 2000 years. Our Fathers passed it down, generation after generations.

**"Be wise to read it all do not add or take anything away."**

# OBSOLETE

## 2 Corinthians 5:17 (AB)

*Therefore if any person is [engrafted] in Christ (the Messiah) he is a new creation (a new creature altogether); the old [previous moral and spiritual condition] has passed away. Behold the fresh and new has come!*

Father, I thank you with my whole heart that you are more than the words that I mutter. You are worthy of the fruit of my lips, for your goodness and your love for me is everlasting. The Lord, because of the Holy Spirit, has given us the opportunity to start a new life. When you really think about what God has done, it literally should astound you. You see He devised this plan knowing that we would mess up. He put strategies in place to ensure without a doubt, that we would eventually find our way back to Him. Thank Him for Jesus! Can you imagine, if all there was for us to look forward to, was just to live here on earth, then die and be buried six feet under? However, because He loves us so much, He really wants to spend eternity with us. Here is where we should be even more grateful. No one knows your stuff better than He does, and in spite of all He knows, it did not stop Him from sending His only Son, to die for us. Pause for just a moment, think of what Christ did on the cross concerning you. Is there anyone in your life that you can think of, that only knows what you've allowed them to know about you, that if you said, in order for me to live forever, I need you to die for me a horrible humiliating death? I don't know of anyone, nor would I be willing to ask anyone, since I know the matter's He took to the cross for me.

### Obsolete:
Dead, gone, extinct, and kaput
That's what happened to the old you and me. All while we were yet in our stuff. What a mighty awesome God we serve, that He would take the old me and make me brand new, just so **I** could be in His presence.

**Take a moment to say Thank you, because just like Dinosaurs, who WE used to be is extinct. Simply because we chose to believe in the One who gave us a chance to live eternally with HIM, regardless of who we were when He devised His plan.**

# TIME TO UNDRESS

## 2 Corinthians 12:7 (MSG)

*Because of the extravagance of those revelations, and so I would not get a big head, I was given the gift of a handicap to keep me in constant touch with my limitations. Satan's angel did his best to get me down; what he in fact did was push me to my knees. No danger then of walking around high and mighty! At first, I did not think of it as a gift, and begged God to remove it. Three times, I did that, and then he told me,*
*My grace is enough; it's all you need. My strength comes into its own in your weakness.*
*Once I heard that, I was glad to let it happen. I quit focusing on the handicap and began appreciating the gift. It was a case of Christ's strength moving in on my weakness. Now I take limitations in stride, and with good cheer, these limitations that cut me down to size—abuse, accidents, opposition, bad breaks. I just let Christ take over. The weaker I get, the stronger I become.*

The time for covering up our stuff ends here today, because we have got some work to do, someone to help, some children to raise, some husbands or wives to love, someone to pray for, some places to go, some dreams to birth, some miracles to witness and be apart of. While studying the text it happened in my heart that the Lord said it is time to silence the shouts that cover up our real pain, sometimes we praise aloud so that no one can really hear the cry of the heart. We walk away week after week upset that no one noticed, but how could they, we were uniquely covered with your own fig leaves that we so carefully sewed together ourselves, and we even included a very adoring mask to cover our faces that kept everyone from seeing who we really are. Some may be saying well my praise is what gets my breakthrough yes, while that's true have you even admitted to your self the real matter of your heart, better yet do you even really even remember? You know the thing that the bible describes as the thorn in the flesh, the thing that came to take you *out*. My plea to you is this, take it all off, get undressed you will not be alone, tell shyness to back up, today you will liberate yourself and someone else.

All you have to do is be exposed to you and allow the Master to do the rest.

**"Locating your Thorn will be easier once you are undressed."**

# PRAYER OF SALVATION

## 2 Corinthians 6:2 (NKJV)

*For He says:*
*" In an acceptable time I have heard you,*
*And in the day of salvation I have helped you."*

*Behold, now is the accepted time; behold, now is the day of salvation.*

Father, I confess that I am a sinner. I ask that you would come into my heart and save me and that you would give me the opportunity to live eternally with you. I recognize that Jesus Christ, your only Son died that I might live. Lord cleanse me from all unrighteousness, and forgive me for all the sins I so willingly committed against you. Father, I thank you for my salvation, and I thank you for your grace, and mercy that I have been given. Now Jesus come into my heart, make me a new creature. Create in me a new heart and renew a steadfast spirit, that I will follow you all the days of my life. Lord I thank you, that as I rejoice because of my new life, the Angels in heaven rejoice along with me! Jesus, thank you for your blood, that from this moment on will cover me and keep me from the snares of the devil.

## Acts 4:12 (NIV))

*"Salvation is found in no one else, for there is no other name under heaven given to men by  which we must be saved."*

## BIBLE TRANSLATION/ABBREVIATIONS REFERENCE

| ABBREVIATION | TRANSLATION |
| --- | --- |
| (AB) | The Amplified Bible |
| (ESV) | English Standard Version |
| (GNT) | Good News Translation |
| (KJV) | King James Version |
| (NCV) | New Century Version |
| (NIV) | New International Version |
| (NKJV) | New King James Version |
| (MSG) | The Message Bible |

# ABOUT THE AUTHOR

Theresa Kirk, a minister of the Gospel of Jesus Christ was encouraged by her sister, a youth Pastor to write her first book, ***Some Things Made Plain.*** Minister Kirk is currently a coordinator of the women's ministry at her church, Living Praise Christian Center in Chatsworth and Lancaster, California, under the leadership of Pastors, Dr. Fred and Linda Hodge. Previously, as a member of New Beginnings Christian Center in Lancaster, California, under the leadership of Pastors Robert and Stella Quintanar, Raymond and Marilyn Hernandez, she vigorously participated in the women's ministry.

She lives in Palmdale, California with her husband, Ron W. Kirk and two amazing children, daughter, Chelsea and son Jaylon.

# NOTES

# NOTES

# NOTES